Day Hike!

NORTH CASCADES

3rd Edition

Day Hike!

NORTH CASCADES

3rd Edition

Mike McQuaide

SASQUATCH BOOKS
SEATTLE

Printed in China

Published by Sasquatch Books
18 17 16 15 14   10 9 8 7 6 5 4 3 2 1

Cover photograph: Jerry Sanchez
Cover design: Hillary Grant/Joyce Hwang
Interior photographs: Mike McQuaide. Additional photo by Jerry Sanchez (page 189)
Interior maps: Marlene Blair
Interior design: Andrew Fuller/Anna Goldstein
Interior composition: Sarah Plein

Library of Congress Cataloging-in-Publication Data is available.

ISBN: 978-1-57061-846-8

IMPORTANT NOTE: Please use common sense. No guidebook can act as a substitute
for experience, careful planning, the right equipment, and appropriate training.
There is inherent danger in all activities described in this book, and readers
must assume full responsibility for their own actions and safety. Changing or
unfavorable conditions in weather, roads, trails, snow, waterways, and so forth
cannot be anticipated by the author or publisher, but should be considered by
any outdoor participants. The author and publisher will not be responsible for the
safety of the users of this guide.

Sasquatch Books
1904 Third Avenue, Suite 710
Seattle, WA 98101
(206) 467-4300
www.sasquatchbooks.com
custserv@sasquatchbooks.com

CONTENTS

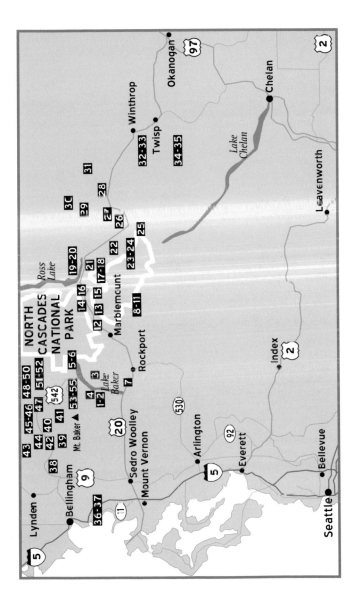

NORTH CASCADES NATIONAL PARK

Ross Lake

Lake Baker

Lake Chelan

Lynden

Bellingham

Mt. Baker ▲

Sedro Woolley

Mount Vernon

Arlington

Everett

Seattle

Bellevue

Rockport

Marblemount

Index

Chelan

Leavenworth

Twisp

Winthrop

Okanogan

36-37

38

43

44

45-46

47

48-50

51-52

5&2

41

42

40

39

1-2

4

3

5-6

53-55

7

8-11

12

13

14

15

16

17-18

19-20

21

22

23-24

25

26

27

28

29

30

31

32-33

34-35

9

20

5

530

92

11

5

2

2

97

HIKES AT A GLANCE

EASY

NO.	HIKE NAME	RATING	BEST SEASON	KIDS	DOGS
4.	Shadow of the Sentinels Trail	★★	Year-round	✔	✔
5.	Baker River Trail	★★★	Year-round	✔	✔
13.	Skagit River Loop	★★	Year-round	✔	✔
20.	Happy Creek Forest Walk	★★	July–Oct	✔	✔
24.	Rainy Lake	★★★	July–Oct	✔	✔
26.	Washington Pass Overlook	★★★★	April–Nov	✔	✔
30.	Slate Peak	★★★	Aug–Oct	✔	✔
40.	Boyd Creek Interpretive Trail	★★	Year-round	✔	✔
42.	Horseshoe Bend Trail	★★	Year-round	✔	✔
53.	Picture Lake	★★★	July–Oct	✔	✔
54.	Bagley Lakes–Lower Wild Goose Trails Loop	★★★	July–Oct	✔	✔
57.	Artist Ridge Trail	★★★★	July–Oct	✔	✔

MODERATE

NO.	HIKE NAME	RATING	BEST SEASON	KIDS	DOGS
1.	Park Butte–Railroad Grade	★★★★★	July–Oct	✔	✔
2.	Scott Paul Trail	★★★	Aug–Oct		✔
6.	Baker Lake Trail	★★★	Year-round	✔	✔
7.	Sauk Mountain	★★★	July–Oct	✔	✔
15.	Pyramid Lake Trail	★★★	Year-round		✔
16.	Diablo Lake Trail	★★★	Year-round		✔
17.	Thunder Knob Trail	★★★	Year-round	✔	✔
19.	Ross Dam	★★★	May–Oct	✔	✔
21.	Ruby Creek Trail	★★	May–Oct	✔	✔
23.	Lake Ann–Maple Pass Loop	★★★★★	July–Oct		✔
25.	Blue Lake Trail	★★★★	July–Oct	✔	✔
27.	Cutthroat Pass Trail	★★★★★	July–Oct	✔	✔

No.	Hike Name	Rating	Best Season	Kids	Dogs
29.	Grasshopper Pass	★★★★★	Aug–Oct		✔
36.	Bat Caves	★★★	Year-round		✔
37.	Fragrance Lake	★★★	Year-round	✔	✔
38.	Canyon Lake	★★★	July–Oct		✔
39.	Heliotrope Ridge Trail	★★★★★	July–Oct		✔
41.	Skyline Divide Trail	★★★★★	July–Oct		✔
44.	Damfino Lakes and Excelsior Mountain	★★★★	July–Oct	✔	✔
49.	Winchester Mountain Lookout	★★★★	July–Oct	✔	✔
50.	High Pass Trail	★★★★	July–Oct	✔	✔
55.	Chain Lakes Loop	★★★★★	July–Oct		✔
56.	Lake Ann Trail	★★★★★	Aug–Oct	✔	✔
58.	Table Mountain	★★★★	July–Oct		

MODERATELY DIFFICULT

No.	Hike Name	Rating	Best Season	Kids	Dogs
3.	Anderson Butte–Watson and Anderson Lakes	★★★★	July–Oct	✔	✔
32.	Sun Mountain Trails	★★★★	Spring/fall	✔	
33.	Patterson Mountain	★★★	Spring/fall	✔	✔
35.	Lookout Mountain Trail (near Twisp)	★★★	Late spring/early fall	✔	✔

DIFFICULT

No.	Hike Name	Rating	Best Season	Kids	Dogs
9.	Hidden Lake Lookout	★★★★★	July–Oct		✔
11.	Cascade Pass–Sahale Arm	★★★★★	July–Oct		
12.	Thornton Lakes–Trappers Peak	★★★★★	July–Oct		
18.	Thunder Creek–Fourth of July Pass	★★★	March–Oct		✔
22.	Easy Pass	★★★★★	July–Oct		✔
28.	Driveway Butte	★★★	March–May		✔
31.	Goat Peak Lookout	★★★★	July–Oct	✔	✔
34.	Slate Creek Trail	★★★★	Late spring/fall		✔
43.	Church Mountain	★★★★	July–Oct		✔
45.	High Divide Trail via Damfino Lakes Trail	★★★★★	July–Oct		✔
46.	Excelsior Pass Trail	★★★	July–Oct		✔

No.	Hike Name	Rating	Best Season	Kids	Dogs
48.	Yellow Aster Butte	★ ★ ★ ★ ★	July–Oct		✔
51.	Goat Mountain	★ ★ ★ ★ ★	July–Oct	✔	✔
52.	Hannegan Pass and Peak	★ ★ ★ ★ ★	July–Oct	✔	✔
59.	Ptarmigan Ridge Trail	★ ★ ★ ★ ★	Aug–Oct		✔

EXTREME

NO.	HIKE NAME	RATING	BEST SEASON	KIDS	DOGS
8.	Lookout Mountain Trail (near Marblemount)	★ ★ ★	July–Oct		✔
10.	Boston Basin	★ ★ ★	July–Oct		
14.	Sourdough Mountain Trail	★ ★ ★	June–Oct		
47.	Welcome Pass	★ ★ ★	July–Oct		✔

ACKNOWLEDGMENTS

A huge shout-out of thanks, gratitude, and appreciation to the following individuals and organizations for offering their support, expertise, and friendship: Bud Hardwick, Jim Kuresman, Doug McKeever, Tim Schultz, Frank Schultz, Paul Ricci, Rick Lingbloom, the Steeles, Margaret Gerard, Washington Trails Association, the *Seattle Times*, and of course, the fine people at Sasquatch Books.

THE NORTH CASCADES

The Cascade Range stretches all the way from the Fraser River in lower British Columbia south to Northern California. For the purposes of this book, however, the North Cascades will be defined as that section of the range from Highway 20/North Cascades Highway north to the US-Canada border. Also included are a couple trails in the Chuckanuts, which some people define as the only place along the coast where the Cascades connect to the sea. Still others say they're not technically part of the range, but then again, who cares? They're beautiful places with terrific trails offering stunning views of islands, mountains, forests, and Puget Sound.

There are two sides, literally, to the North Cascades. The west side puts on a bit of a wet face. Clouds rolling in from the ocean tend to dump most of their moisture on the west side of the Cascade crest—elevation, about 5,000 feet—before they ever make it to the east side. From November to April, this means snow—so much snow, in fact, that during the 1998–99 snow season, a world record 1,140 inches of snow—that's 95 feet—fell at the Mount Baker ski area, about 40 miles east of Bellingham. The rest of the year those clouds offer much in the way of rain, showers, drizzle, mizzle, fog, and precip. Though from mid-July to the end of August, they do seem to give it a rest and there's no finer place in the world than the west side of the North Cascades. Because of the heavy precip, you'll not only run into more snow on the west side but also be more apt to tickle the toes of glaciers, which are more prevalent here than anyplace else in the Lower 48. Not surprisingly, waterfalls—that's why they're called the Cascades after all—and water in general are more plentiful on the west side too.

With the clouds mostly rained and snowed out by the time they cross the crest, the east side enjoys less snow and rain than the west, thus more sunny days. In a typical year, mountain trails on the east side are clear of snow a little earlier in the year than those on the west.

Common trees in the North Cascades include western red cedar, western hemlock, Douglas fir, and Pacific silver fir, with the east side of the Cascades boasting ponderosa pine, Engelmann spruce, and subalpine and western larch. Several trails in this book offer walks among trees more than 500 years old.

Being a day hiking guide, this book won't even pretend to be a comprehensive guide to Northwest flora and fauna; critter-wise and plant-wise, the species are too numerous to describe. However, some of the common folk worth a mention include bald eagle, osprey, black bear, Roosevelt elk, mountain lion, hoary marmot, pika, mountain goats, American dipper, and ravens. Among the plants you're likely to see are trillium, Indian paintbrush, subalpine lupine, mountain heather, columbine, devil's club, huckleberries, blueberries, and more fungis and algae than you can shake a hundred sticks at.

National Park/National Forest/Recreation Areas

Established in 1968, North Cascades National Park Service Complex is a half-million-acre paradise of jagged mountain peaks, glacier-clad crags, cascading waterfalls, otherworldly forests, and seemingly everything in between. That said, only about a third of the trails in this book enter the national park. Despair not. The lands surrounding the national park complex—Mount Baker–Snoqualmie and Okanogan–Wenatchee National Forests, which include a number of wilderness and recreation areas—are themselves paradises of jagged mountain peaks, cascading waterfalls, glacier-clad crags, otherworldly forests, and seemingly everything in between.

Hiking is free on both national park and national forest trails, but parking isn't. To park at most of the trailheads in this book (unless the description says otherwise), day hikers need a Northwest Forest Pass. Forest passes cost $5 for a daily pass, $30 for an annual. They're available at National Forest Ranger stations, REI stores and various retail outlets throughout the Puget Sound region, and online at www.usgs.gov. Click "buy recreation passes." (There is no fee to enter North Cascades National Park.)

Those 62 and older are eligible for an Interagency Senior Pass, a $10 lifetime pass that's honored at any federal site (e.g. national forests, national parks, etc.) that charges entry fees. It's available at the same outlets listed for the Northwest Forest Pass above.

In addition, state parks now require a Discover Pass. It costs $10 for a daily pass, $30 for an annual, and is available at various retail outlets and online at www.discoverpass.wa.gov.

Day hikers do need to note some differences between national park and national forest trails. Leashed dogs are allowed on national forest trails (except Picture Lake and Table Mountain), but not on many national park trails. In general, they're allowed in Ross Lake National Recreation Area (which is part of North Cascades National Park Complex) but not in North Cascades National Park trails proper. It's a bit confusing and on some trails—e.g., Sourdough Mountain, which begins in the Ross Lake National Recreation Area but crosses into the national park proper land—leashed dogs are allowed on part of, but not the whole trail. (On trails such as this, a sign or post designates where you cross into national park land.) The individual trail descriptions that follow will fill you in on details. Mountain bikes are not allowed on national park trails or on most national forest trails. Again, check the following trail descriptions for details.

USING THIS GUIDE

The beginning of each trail description is intended to give you quick information that can help you decide whether the specific day hike is one that interests you. Here's what you'll find:

Trail Number & Name

Trails are numbered in this guide following a geographical order; see the Overview Map on page vii for general location. Trail names usually reflect those names used by the national park, national forest service, and other land managers. In some cases, portions of very long trails or multiple sections of separate trails may have been combined into a single hike and assigned a new name.

Overall Rating

Because it's so subjective, assigning an overall rating to a hike can be a difficult task because of that whole different-strokes-for-different-folks phenomenon. That said, because I hiked all the trails and have opinions about which ones I liked, which ones I liked a lot, which ones I loved, and which ones I loved and never wanted to leave, assigning ratings wasn't that hard.

So that the ratings make sense to you, I'll explain what kinds of things turn my trekking poles up to eleven and thus were likely to make me rate a particular trail higher than another.

In general, trails in dense forest, with no mountain vistas, rate lower than those with mountain views. I love the dense Northwest forests as much as anyone, but because this is a book about the North Cascades, the trails with the mountain vistas are the ones that rate the highest. Water features, whether they be rushing rivers, cascading waterfalls, or peaceful alpine lakes, raise a trail's rating, as do wildflower meadows. Lack of crowds is a plus too.

Trails that rate the highest are those that fire on all cylinders. For example, you might pass through old-growth forest, cross meadows splashed with Indian paintbrush and myriad wildflowers, climb to an alpine environment where you're surrounded by mountains, ridges, and glaciers, and finally, after a short rock scramble, reach an old fire lookout that stares down onto a peaceful mountain lake. Hidden Lake Lookout (Hike 9) is a good example.

With the above in mind, trails are rated from one to five, with five reserved for the most spectacular ones.

★ This hike is worth taking, even with your in-laws.

★★ Expect to discover socially and culturally redeeming values on this hike. Or, at least, very fine scenery.

★★★ You would be willing to get up before sunrise to take this hike, even if you watched all of Letterman the night before.

★★★★ Here is the Häagen-Dazs of hikes; if you don't like ice cream, a hike with this rating will give more pleasure than any favorite comfort food.

★★★★★ The aesthetic and physical rewards are so great that hikes given this rating are forbidden by most conservative religions.

Distance

The distance listed is round-trip, exclusive of any side trips to Really Big Trees or other features mentioned along the way. If these excursions off the main trail are longer than about 0.2 miles, that distance will be mentioned in the description of the hike. The distances given are the best estimates I could come up with. Determining distances on trails is difficult, as maps are not always accurate and are often at odds with trail signs and other maps.

Hiking Time

This is an estimate of the time it takes the average hiker to walk the trail, round-trip. Since none of us are average hikers, feel free to ignore this entry. For the most part, however, the pace on the trail is calculated at 2 to 3 miles per hour, depending on how flat or steep a trail is. Times are estimated conservatively; even so, this rate might slow on trails with significant elevation gain.

Elevation Gain

This is the trail's cumulative elevation gain. Not all of it will be gained on the way to your destination. Some trails actually lose elevation on the way and gain it on the return, or alternately gain and lose elevation along the way. The certainty is that on a round-trip hike, you always gain the same amount of elevation that you lose.

High Point

This is the highest point above sea level you'll reach on any given hike.

Difficulty Level

Here's where you'll find how much effort you'll expend hiking a particular trail. Hills, how primitive a trail is, length, and elevation gain were all taken into consideration. Like the overall rating, this is very subjective. Experienced hikers will likely find a hike rated "Moderately Difficult" to be only "Moderate," while beginning trekkers might rate the same hike "Difficult." As with the hiking times, noted above, the difficulty of individual hikes were rated conservatively.

Trail difficulty is rated from one to five, with five being reserved for hikers with high endurance seeking the greatest challenge.

♦ Easy: Few, if any, hills; generally between 1 and 4 miles, round-trip; suitable for families with small children.

♦♦ Moderate: Longer, gently graded hills; generally 4 to 6 miles long, round-trip.

♦♦♦ Steeper grades; elevation changes greater than about 1,000 feet; between 6 and 9 miles long, round-trip.

♦♦♦♦ Moderately Difficult: Sustained, steep climbs of at least 1 mile; elevation gain and loss greater than 1,500 feet; usually more than 9 miles long, round-trip.

♦♦♦♦♦ Extreme: Sustained steep climbs; distances greater than 10 miles, round-trip. These trails are high on the lung-busting, thigh-burning, knee-crunching scale and will put your hiking skills to the test.

Best Season

Here you'll find our recommendation for the best time of year to take any given hike. Trails that are open throughout the year or that make good three-season hikes will be noted here.

Permits/Contact

This entry will tell you whether you need a Northwest Forest Pass or other permit and which land manager to contact for more information.

Maps

The two most popular types of maps, United States Geological Survey (USGS) "quads" and Green Trails, are listed for each hike where applicable. The appropriate Amazing Maps for the two hikes in the Chuckanuts are included as well. Maps are available at outdoor retailers, park visitor centers, and other sources. Smartphone and tablet users can also take advantage of the myriad trail map apps now available.

Each hike in this book includes a trail map of the route, featuring parking and trailhead, alternate routes, direction, elevation profile, and more. Our maps are based most often on USGS; use the legend on page xix.

Trail Notes

Look here for a quick guide to trail regulations and features: leashed dogs okay; off-leash dogs okay; no dogs; bikes allowed; kid-friendly; good views.

After the at-a-glance overview of each hike, you'll find detailed descriptions of the following:

The Hike

This section attempts to convey the feel of the hike in a few sentences; it includes the type of trail and whether the views are jaw-dropping or just simply grand.

Getting There

Here's where you'll find driving directions to the trailhead from the nearest major highway. The trailhead elevation is also included.

The main access highways for all but two of these hikes are Highway 20 (North Cascades Highway) and Highway 542 (Mount

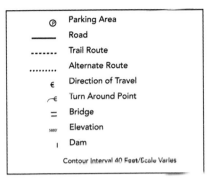

℗	Parking Area
——	Road
·······	Trail Route
········	Alternate Route
€	Direction of Travel
⌐€	Turn Around Point
=	Bridge
5880'	Elevation
⏐	Dam

Contour Interval 40 Feet/Scale Varies

Baker Highway) Highway 20 heads east from I-5 at Burlington, about 60 miles north of Seattle. Most of the Highway 20-accessed trails in this book are found between mileposts 82 and 179, ranging from 20 to 120 miles east of Burlington.

Highway 542 heads east from I-5 at Bellingham, about 90 miles north of Seattle. All but one of the Highway 542-accessed trails are found from milepost 34 (34 miles east of Bellingham) to the road's end at about milepost 58.

The Trail

Here's the blow by-blow, mile-by-mile description of each trail. Along with route descriptions, you'll find what to look forward to—awesome views, killer uphills, easy-to-miss turnoffs, and so forth. Distances to selected intersections and landmarks along the way are also included.

Going Farther

In this section, you can learn about good options for extending the hike along the same trail. Interesting side trips can be found here, too. And if there's a nearby campground that could get you on the trail sooner, it also will be mentioned. Not every hike includes this section.

BE CAREFUL

It is all too easy on a warm, sunny day on the trail to forget all of the stuff you ought to be carrying in your pack. Day hikers, especially, are likely to leave that extra layer or Gore-Tex parka in the trunk. Some folks even forget that most essential item—a hiking partner. Never hike alone.

Virtually every time, day hikers who forget one or two of the basic rules for safe wilderness travel return to the trailhead smiling and healthy. No trail cop is going to cite you for negligent hiking if you have only nine of the so-called "Ten Essentials," or if you hit the trail without registering or telling someone where you're going.

Perhaps the only weighty argument anyone can make to convince another day hiker to follow the rules for safe travel in the outdoors is this: Remember the annual, avoidable tragedies that occur because hikers ignore those rules and become news headlines instead.

The Ten Essentials

No matter the distance or difficulty of the hike, always carry the Ten Essentials in your pack.

- A topographic **map** of the area.
- A **compass**, and the ability to use it in conjunction with the map. Portable GPS units are excellent aids to navigation, but can't always be depended on in areas of heavy tree cover. Also, they require batteries, which can fail.
- **Extra clothing**, consisting of a top and bottom insulating layer and a waterproof and windproof top layer. A hat or cap is also a necessity.
- A one-day supply of **water** and **extra food** that requires no cooking. Energy bars, jerky, or dried fruits work well.
- Carry a **flashlight** with extra batteries and bulbs; a headlamp is a good option. Many of these lights have spare bulbs built-in. Lithium batteries, though more expensive, make excellent spares because of their long shelf-life.

- Excellent **first-aid kits** that come already assembled are available on the market. Make sure your kit includes wraps for sprains and some kind of blister treatment.
- **Matches** in a waterproof case are recommended over butane lighters, as both altitude and temperature can affect a lighter's performance.
- Candles work well as a **fire starter**, along with a variety of lightweight commercial products.
- A **pocketknife** is an indispensable tool.
- **Sunglasses** and **sunscreen** are important, especially at high altitudes or when the ground is snow-covered.

In addition to these items, most day hikers never hit the trail without tucking some toilet paper in a plastic bag and perhaps some type of bug repellent on summer hikes. A loud emergency whistle is a lightweight addition. A small, insulating "space blanket" makes a nice lunch tablecloth—and could save your life if you have to spend the night. Binoculars are worth their weight simply for watching wildlife, and might help you find your route if you become lost. Consider, too, trekking poles or a walking stick of some variety; it can take the stress off your knees on steep downhills, help steady you while crossing streams, and serve a wide variety of other useful purposes, such as a support post for a portable lean-to should you need emergency shelter.

Water

Dehydration is one of the most common ailments that day hikers face. No one should head out on the trail without at least one liter of clean water per person. As stated earlier, the west side of the North Cascades is a very wet place, and finding water to filter or pill before drinking shouldn't be a problem. East of Washington Pass, it's a different story, especially in high summer. If creeks and lakes along the trail are scarce and finding water might be a problem, it's usually mentioned in the trail description.

Treat all water in the wilderness as if it were contaminated. The most worrisome problem might be a little critter called Giardia lamblia, which can give you a case of the trots that you'll never forget. The most noticeable symptom of giardiasis is "explosive diarrhea." Need you know more? Probably not.

Thankfully, there is an easy way to assure that the water you take from mountain streams and lakes is safe to drink. When used properly, filter pumps eliminate at least 99.9 percent of giardia and other dangerous organisms from the water. A recent and far more convenient addition to filter pumps, especially for day hikers, are relatively inexpensive water bottles equipped with their own filters. You simply fill the bottle from the stream (taking extreme care not to contaminate the mouthpiece or drinking cap), drop the filter into place, screw on the top, and you're ready to drink filtered water. Conversely, many veteran hikers still choose to forego all this gadgetry and use the old-fashioned method: iodine water treatments, which come in tablets or crystals. The taste might be objectionable to some, but it's a guaranteed way to kill giardia and other waterborne bugs—something a filter, especially an improperly used or maintained one, is not.

Weather

Northwest weather can be highly unpredictable, especially at higher elevations. An old salt once told me that above 5,000 feet, there's the potential for winter every single day of the year. He knew what of he spoke too, for he told me this on a summer night when we were huddled in a tent at the toe of Mount Baker's Easton Glacier during a raging snowstorm blowing 30mph winds. Then again, especially on the warmer east side of the Cascades, some summer days can be so sunny and bright that sunstroke is a concern.

On both sides of the Cascades, weather can change rapidly and with little warning. On an alpine hike in the fall, you could get snowed upon, rained upon, sleeted upon, blown around, and finally sunburned—all in the span of a day. Hikers in Washington's mountains have frozen to death in July and drowned in the afternoon while fording flood-filled rivers that were shallow in the morning.

Of course, all elevations offer the potential for rain, and where there's rain, wind, and cool temperatures, hypothermia is a real threat. Waterproof, windproof gear can be life-saving in such situations.

Treat hypothermia by doing the following: Get the person out of the rain, cold, and wind immediately. Remove all wet clothing. Because hypothermia victims are often dehydrated, have them drink plenty of fluids. Get them indoors as soon as possible but remember that gradual rewarming of the victim is advisable. Rewarming that is too abrupt can strain the hypothermic person's heart. To prevent hypothermia, know the weather conditions and forecast, and always carry extra clothes.

To be safe, always call the appropriate land manager or check their websites for the latest trail conditions, including snow levels.

Flora & Fauna

For the most part, the animals and plants of the Cascades are benign. The most common danger might be an encounter with poison oak or stinging nettles. However, in rare instances, a hiker might encounter a rattlesnake, black bear, or (most rare) a cougar.

Day hikers needn't fear black bears, but realize these are wild animals that can cause serious injury if provoked. While there are few (if any) grizzly bears to worry about, research indicates that a black bear attack, though extremely rare, may lead more often to a fatality. A greater potential danger might be from cougars. Encounters between humans and cougars are believed to be increasing throughout Washington State, but you probably will never see one on the trail.

If you do encounter a bear or cougar, heed the following advice from the Department of Fish and Wildlife:

Bear: Give the bear plenty of room to get away. Never get between a cub and its mother. Avoid eye contact but speak softly to the bear while backing away from it. Try not to show fear and don't turn your back on a bear. If you can't get away from it, clap your hands or yell in an effort to scare it away. If the bear becomes aggressive, fight back using anything at your disposal. Should the attack continue, curl up in a ball or lay down on your stomach and play dead.

Cougar: Don't take your eyes off the cougar. Make yourself appear big by raising your arms above your head, open your jacket if you're wearing one, and wave a stick above your head. If the cougar approaches, yell and throw rocks, sticks, or anything you can get your hands on. In the event of an attack, fight back aggressively.

Rattlesnake: Most of the time, if you come across a rattlesnake, it will slither away, but if not, give it plenty of room—about 10 feet—and walk around it. Rattlers can strike up to 4 feet, and although sometimes their bites are dry, it's not the type of thing that you should take a chance with. If bitten, seek medical treatment as soon as possible.

Less dangerous, but more common hazards to day hikers include stinging and biting pests such as yellow jackets, particularly in late summer and early fall, and black flies, mosquitoes and deer flies. Liberal doses of insect repellent can take care of the mosquitoes and deer flies, but probably won't keep those pesky yellow jackets away.

Poison oak and ivy grow in some areas of the Cascades, mostly in sunny, dry areas. A more common plant pest is stinging nettle, which grows in profusion along many trails.

Etiquette/Ethics

To protect this wonderful landscape so that users in future generations can enjoy it just as much as you, please follow a few simple rules. Stay on established trails, don't cut switchbacks, and stay off sensitive areas. Leave no trace, pack out your trash, and respect other trail users. And because you're having such a great time using Washington's trails, why not volunteer your services by lending a hand on a trail building or repair project?

Happy trails! ■

BAKER LAKE

---

1. Park Butte–Railroad Grade

RATING	DISTANCE	HIKING TIME
★ ★ ★ ★ ★	7 to 9 miles round-trip	3 to 6 hours
ELEVATION GAIN	HIGH POINT	DIFFICULTY
1,800 to 2,150 feet	5,400 feet	♦ ♦ ♦ ♦ ♦
BEST SEASON		
Jan Feb Mar Apr May Jun Jul Aug Sep Oct Nov Dec		

The Hike

A visit to a spiff lookout and the chance to peer deeply down a glacial moraine are just a couple of the features of this popular hike that offers big-time south-side Baker views. It's cheesy, but fun, to say—Park Butte is truly a beaut.

Getting There

Head east on Highway 20 (North Cascades Highway) to milepost 82.3, about 15 miles east of Sedro-Woolley. Turn left on Baker Lake Road. About 12.5 miles farther, turn left onto Forest Road 12. In 3 miles, turn right on FR 13 and follow it for 6 miles to the road-end parking lot. Elevation: 3,300 feet.

The Trail

Start by following the obvious trail heading to the right from the trailhead map kiosk. About 100 yards ahead, bear left at the sign for the Scott Paul Trail (Hike 2)—a delight in its own right—and cross

PERMITS/CONTACT
Northwest Forest Pass required/Mount Baker National Recreation Area, (360) 856-5700

MAPS
USGS Baker Pass; Green Trails Hamilton 45

TRAIL NOTES
Leashed dogs okay; kid-friendly; raging river views

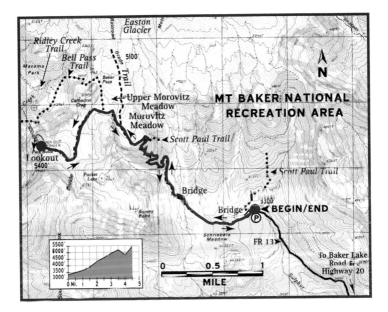

Sulphur Creek via a wooden bridge. Soon walk a mix of dirt trail and boardwalk through relatively flat Schreibers Meadow, a heathered, wildflower-strewn spot complete with ponds and connecting exploratory paths. Look north and see Mount Baker's Sherman Peak, the pointy nubbin on Baker's south side.

After entering forest, the trail becomes a little rockier and narrower and, at **0.9** mile, reaches a bouldery creek area, the end result of numerous volcanic mudflows. Trekking poles are strongly advised here. Cross a suspension bridge and eventually return to forest. Switchback steeply and at **2.0** miles, at the intersection with the Scott Paul Trail (Hike 2, once again) take a left, following the sign for Park Butte.

Just ahead, emerge into lovely Morovitz Meadow, where everything—mountain views, wildflower power, and blueberry succulence—is ratcheted up a notch. Enjoy, then proceed. At about **2.3** miles is the signed intersection with the Railroad Grade Trail,

Pocket of fog above Pocket Lake

where you must choose your next destination. The Railroad Grade description follows the one for Park Butte.

For Park Butte: At the signed intersection with the Railroad Grade Trail at about **2.3** miles, go left. Reach the mostly flat—and damp—Upper Morovitz Meadow in about 0.5 mile. The trail swings west and then south, climbing steeply up a rocky, bouldery, almost moonscape-spooky area. Above and to the right is your lookout destination; to the left is Railroad Grade, which earns its name from its steady, even, straight-line grade. After crossing a (likely) snowfield, the trail swings northwest again, offering terrific views of the reddish Twin Sisters Range, and at **3.5** miles, stops at Park Butte Lookout, at the boundary of the Mount Baker Wilderness. Views are beyond stunning, and the lookout itself, available for camping on a first-come, first-served basis, is truly a room with a view. Return the same way.

For Railroad Grade: At the intersection with the Railroad Grade sign in Morovitz Meadow at about **2.3** miles, proceed up an approximately 0.25-mile flight of stone plank steps. When you crest a ridge, bear right, and after passing a number of not-so-private campsites (careful not to knock over someone's tent), reach the amazing moraine in about 0.5 mile. A raging creek, the meltwater of Easton Glacier, snakes through at the bottom, and across the way to the east you can see the Scott Paul Trail (Hike 2, again), another adventure for another day. Follow the trail as far as the snow level allows, about 0.75 mile from the trail junction. Eventually it diminishes to a climbers' path to the Easton Glacier. (Note: This is the access route for one of the most popular Mount Baker climbing routes.) Return the same way.

Going Farther

Other nearby trails accessed near Upper Morovitz Meadow include Scott Paul Trail (Hike 2), as well as the Ridley Creek, Bell Pass, and Elbow Lake Trails.

Campsites can be found at the trailhead, at Upper Morovitz Meadow, and at a couple of points along the Railroad Grade Trail. Park Butte Lookout is available on a first-come, first-served basis. ■

2. Scott Paul Trail

RATING	DISTANCE	HIKING TIME
★★★☆☆	7.5-mile loop	5 hours
ELEVATION GAIN	**HIGH POINT**	**DIFFICULTY**
1,800 feet	5,050 feet	◆◆◇◇◇

BEST SEASON
Jan Feb Mar Apr May Jun Jul **Aug Sep Oct** Nov Dec

The Hike

This fun loop offers a terrific south-side tour of Mount Baker, first through meadow and forest, then across a rugged glacial moraine environment. Mountain views are huge, but snow lingers long here—especially on the northernmost 3-mile stretch—so check with the ranger for the latest conditions. This recently constructed gem is named in honor of Scott Paul, a popular Forest Service employee who conceived of the trail but was killed in a bridge-building accident before its completion.

Getting There

Head east on Highway 20 (North Cascades Highway) to milepost 82.3, about 15 miles east of Sedro-Woolley. Turn left on Baker Lake Road. About 12.5 miles farther, turn left on Forest Road 12. In 3 miles, turn right on FR 13 and follow it for 6 miles to the road-end parking lot. Elevation: 3,300 feet.

PERMITS/CONTACT
Northwest Forest Pass required/Mount Baker National Recreation Area, (360) 856-5700

MAPS
USGS Baker Pass; Green Trails Hamilton 45

TRAIL NOTES
Leashed dogs okay; great views

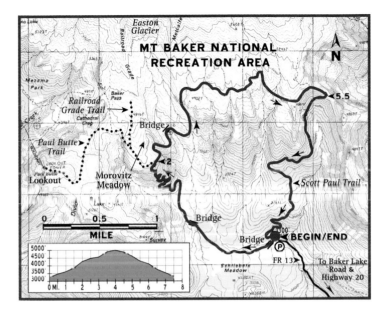

The Trail

For the first 2 miles, this hike follows the same trail as Hike 1, Park Butte–Railroad Grade; follow that description, and note: about 100 yards past the trailhead, at the Scott Paul Trail sign to the right, go left—to the right is the way from which you'll return. At the second intersection with the Scott Paul Trail, at **2.0** miles, go right on the Scott Paul Trail.

The trail soon exits the forest and traverses meadows of wildflowers that offer the first Mount Baker views. Sherman Peak, the little pointy nubbin on Baker's south side, hardly looks like a nubbin from this angle, but instead resembles the Matterhorn. Soon enter a glacial moraine environment, which, besides up-close and personal views of Baker's Easton and Squak Glaciers, means the trail passes through boulders, rocks, and rushing creeks—and, of course, that your shoes and socks will get soaked. Expect much of the same over the next 3-plus miles.

Sherman Peak on Mount Baker's south side

At **2.7** miles, cross a springy suspension bridge. To your left, Railroad Grade (Hike 1), the aptly named moraine that slants upward in an almost perfectly straight line, stuns with its sheer size. At **3.5** miles the trail turns to the east and levels off (mostly) for about the next 2 miles. Though not much climbing is required, the trail remains rugged with a number of creeks and, most likely, snow patches to cross. At **5.5** miles, the trail leaves the high country and heads south into the woods, returning to the trailhead in about 2 miles.

Going Farther
This is also the same trailhead for Park Butte–Railroad Grade (Hike 1). Camping is allowed at the trailhead. ■

3. Anderson Butte–Watson and Anderson Lakes

RATING	DISTANCE	HIKING TIME
★★★★☆	2.8 to 7 miles round-trip	2 to 5 hours
ELEVATION GAIN	**HIGH POINT**	**DIFFICULTY**
1,000 to 2,000 feet	5,350 feet	◆◆◆◇◇

BEST SEASON
Jan Feb Mar Apr May Jun **Jul Aug Sep Oct** Nov Dec

The Hike

One trail, three destinations. Whether you're a hiker who lusts after lakes or one who ogles peaks, this popular network of trails high above Baker Lake is sure to please. Watson Lakes, Anderson Lakes, and Anderson Butte are so close that if you have time, visit all three. Expect crowds on weekends.

Getting There

Head east on Highway 20 (North Cascades Highway) to milepost 82.3, about 15 miles east of Sedro-Woolley. Turn left on Baker Lake Road and head north. At about 13.8 miles, turn right onto gravel Forest Road 1106 (Baker Lake Dam Road). Cross Baker Dam in about 1.5 miles, and about 0.6 mile after that, turn left on FR 1107.

PERMITS/CONTACT
Northwest Forest Pass required/Mount Baker–Snoqualmie National Forest, (360) 856-5700

MAPS
USGS Bacon Peak; Green Trails Lake Shannon 46

TRAIL NOTES
Leashed dogs okay; kid-friendly; great views

Watson Lake and Bacon Peak

After 9 miles on FR 1107, turn left onto FR 022 and follow the sign for Watson Lakes Trail. The road-end trailhead is 1.1 miles ahead. Elevation: 4,300 feet.

The Trail

Start by ascending steadily through moss-strewn hemlock forest, crossing the occasional wood bridge or steps at particularly mushy spots. At **0.9** mile, just after emerging onto open—and, likely, damp—meadow, reach a signed intersection for the trail to Anderson Butte.

For Anderson Butte: Go left for the butte if you're a peak ogler and resume climbing almost immediately—climbing in earnest at that. You'll gain about 600 feet over the next 0.5 mile, which includes a potentially slippery boulder slide area. At **1.4** miles, reach a notch that pays with spectacular views east—Mount Shuksan, the Picket Range, Bacon Peak, et cetera, not to mention nearby Anderson Butte to your right. Follow the trail along the ridge to the left for a few hundred yards to a rock outcropping, where you can go no farther (unless you have wings). Wraparound views include everything just mentioned, along with Baker Lake, the pinkish Twin Sisters (as well as the rest of the Sisters family), and Mount Baker. Unfortunate views of hillside clearcuts are here too. Return the same way.

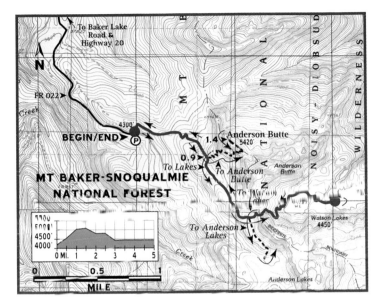

For the lakes: At the intersection with the Anderson Butte Trail at **0.9** mile (1.9 miles if you went to the butte first), go right. Continue down, then up across the damp and flower-strewn meadow, reentering forest after about 0.3 mile. Drop rapidly for a couple hundred yards. Just after exiting the forest, at **1.5** miles from the trailhead (2.5 cumulative miles if you went to the butte first) reach a signed intersection.

For Watson Lakes: Go straight; reenter forest and after a 0.25-mile ascent, reach a small ridge. Then begin dropping steadily into the lake basin. Soon enough, just after you enter the Noisy–Diobsud Wilderness, the lakes come into view, stunning against the glaciated backdrop of Bacon Peak. Go whole hog and attain lakeside magic at the western lake. Explore away, continuing along the north side of the lake to reach the east Watson Lake at about **2.5** miles from the trailhead (3.5 cumulative miles if you went to Anderson Butte first). Return the same way.

For Anderson Lakes: At the signed intersection **1.5** miles from the trailhead (4.5 cumulative miles if you went to Anderson Butte and Watson Lakes first), go right. The lakes are just 0.5 mile of meadow and boulder field away, 2.0 miles from the trailhead (5 cumulative miles if you went to Anderson Butte and Watson Lakes first). Return the same way.

Going Farther

Horseshoe Cove Campground and Kulshan Campground, both near Baker Dam, are just two of the several campgrounds located along both sides of Baker Lake. ■

4. Shadow of the Sentinels Trail

RATING	DISTANCE	HIKING TIME
★★☆☆☆	**0.5-mile loop**	**30 minutes**
ELEVATION GAIN	HIGH POINT	DIFFICULTY
30 feet	**1,020 feet**	◆◇◇◇◇
BEST SEASON		
Jan Feb Mar Apr May Jun Jul Aug Sep Oct Nov Dec		

The Hike

Step out of your car and step back in time on this short, boardwalk-and-asphalt trail that gets you up-close and personal with some of the oldest trees in the area. One, a fir now 7 feet in diameter, was just a sapling when Dante was putting the final touches on that Inferno thing. Lots of interpretive signage.

Getting There

Head east on Highway 20 (North Cascades Highway) to just past milepost 82.3, about 15 miles east of Sedro-Woolley. Turn left on Baker Lake Road. Continue for about 15 miles to the trailhead parking lot on the right. Elevation: 1,000 feet.

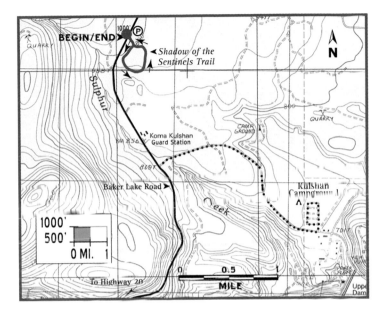

The Trail

The cross-section display in the parking lot of a 500-year-old Douglas fir is just a hint of what you'll see on the forested trail. Thankfully, the trees on the trail are alive—or, if not, they're being useful in their after-lives as nurse logs for other forest flora and fauna.

PERMITS/CONTACT
Northwest Forest Pass required/Mount Baker–Snoqualmie National Forest, (360) 856-5700

MAPS
USGS Welker Peak; Green Trails Lake Shannon 46

TRAIL NOTES
Leashed dogs okay; kid-friendly; wheelchair-accessible

Shadows of ancient trees

The interpretive nature walk starts out on boardwalk. Just past the trail register book, check out the first of the many signs that provide details on the forest life all around you. Sit on one of the benches, look, and listen: woodpeckers, robins, and Steller's jays; massive, moss-draped firs and cedars; owls of one sort or another; maidenhair ferns; maybe even a flying squirrel if you put in the time. Lollygag and saunter—both methods are useful here.

Going Farther

Horseshoe Cove Campground and Kulshan Campground, both less than 2 miles from the trailhead, are just two of the many campgrounds on either side of Baker Lake. ■

5. Baker River Trail

RATING	DISTANCE	HIKING TIME
★★★☆☆	**5.2 miles round-trip**	**3 hours**
ELEVATION GAIN	HIGH POINT	DIFFICULTY
400 feet	**900 feet**	◆◇◇◇◇
BEST SEASON		
Jan Feb Mar Apr May Jun Jul Aug Sep Oct Nov Dec		

The Hike

Sure, this wooded shoulder-season trail is great in winter and on rainy days, but because it also offers some open ridgetop views, it's great anytime of year. The river itself is a stunner—part meandering slow-poke, part rushing rapids—and the forest will have you scratching your head: How can so many massive, ancient cedars grow seemingly right out of granite boulders?

Getting There

Head east on Highway 20 (North Cascades Highway) to just past milepost 82.3, about 15 miles east of Sedro-Woolley. Turn left on Baker Lake Road and head north for 26 miles to the road-end parking lot and the Baker River trailhead. Elevation: 780 feet.

The Trail

From the trailhead, head north on the obvious trail. The first 0.5 mile, which is also the north entrance to the Baker Lake Trail, is flat, wide, and barrier-free—perfect for families and those with disabilities. This section gives a taste of what's to come—an otherworldly jumble of massive cedars and blocky boulders, strung with lichens above and lain with mosses down below, as well as cool, rushing Baker River to the right.

At **0.5** mile, at the intersection with the Baker Lake Trail, continue straight, following the sign for Baker River Trail. The trail immediately narrows to a winding single track that passes around and through

Canopy sky along Baker River

boulders. Just ahead, pass an area where the river, in its snakier moods, occasionally washes out the trail, which requires it to be rerouted.

The trail eventually leaves the riverside, heads up and into the forest, then reemerges about 40 feet above the river at an exciting bend. Emerald whirlpools, mini haystacks, and good old-fashioned rapids promise to entrance you. At **1.2** miles, cross the first of several streams, which offer wet-foot potential. About 0.25 mile ahead, just after an amazing mega-wishbone formed by two cedars, cross a log footbridge over a rushing creek and enter a cool, silent forest of giants, seemingly miles (actually, just a couple hundred yards) away from the Baker River.

PERMITS/CONTACT
Northwest Forest Pass required/Mount Baker–Snoqualmie National Forest, (360) 856-5700

MAPS
USGS Bacon Peak, Mount Shuksan; Green Trails Lake Shannon 46, Mount Shuksan 14

TRAIL NOTES
Leashed dogs okay to national park boundary; kid-friendly

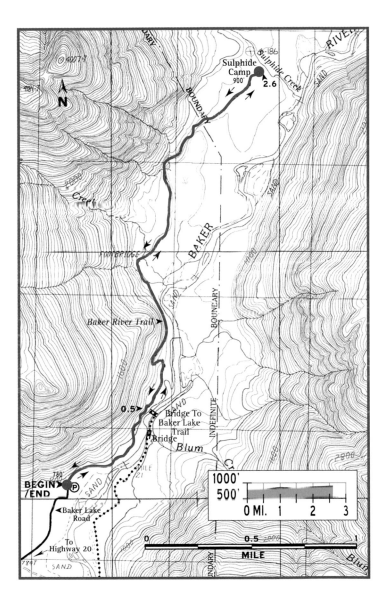

Jagged Ridge above Sulphide Creek

Just after returning to the river, notice how it doesn't seem to be in a rush anymore. In fact, it's standing still, and seems more lakelike than riveresque. That's because it's not really the river but, rather, a massive beaver dam.

At **2.1** miles pass the North Cascades National Park boundary marker and, about 0.5 mile ahead, Sulphide Creek. This rushing gusher of a stream is your turnaround point, as well as a perfect spot for lunch or camping. Sit on the creek's banks at Sulphide Camp while looking up through the clearing to Jagged Ridge on Mount Shuksan's southeast flank. Return the same way.

Going Farther

Camping is available at the trailhead and at Sulphide Camp on Sulphide Creek, as well as at several camps alongside Baker Lake. ∎

6. Baker Lake Trail

RATING	DISTANCE	HIKING TIME
★★★☆☆	9 miles round-trip	5 hours
ELEVATION GAIN	**HIGH POINT**	**DIFFICULTY**
250 feet	980 feet	◆◆◇◇◇
BEST SEASON		
Jan Feb Mar Apr May Jun Jul Aug Sep Oct Nov Dec		

The Hike

Big trees, a couple of big mountains, and one big lake are what you'll find on this year-round, lakeside trail. Oh yeah: several big creeks and a big river, too. This hike explores Baker Lake's north end, where two recently completed bridges now offer passage into this land of old-growth bigness. Much of this trail follows a nineteenth-century lumbering and mining route.

Getting There

Head east on Highway 20 (North Cascades Highway) to just past milepost 82.3, about 15 miles east of Sedro-Woolley. Turn left on Baker Lake Road and head north for 26 miles to the road-end parking lot and the Baker River trailhead, which is where you start. Elevation: 780 feet.

The Trail

First thing, from the parking lot, look high across the river to the rocky cliffs of Hagan Mountain to the east and try to spot tiny white specks. A pair of binoculars reveals those specks to be mountain goats.

Head out on the wide, barrier-free, giant cedar–lined trail as for Hike 5, Baker River Trail. At **0.5** mile, at a signed intersection, follow the trail to the right—Baker Lake Trail No. 610 —over the Baker River via the spiffy, fairly new cable-stay bridge. Once across, after you stop to ogle the river and the amazing river valley that seems to stretch on forever in either direction, the forest walk is a bit more on the wild side. The trail is still easy to follow (though no longer

Cedars along Baker Lake

barrier-free), but the woods are denser, the lichen heavier, the mossy boulders woollier.

In a couple hundred yards, cross rushing, roaring, and icy Blum Creek via another new bridge. A study in minor ups and downs, the trail slaloms through big trees with the Baker River—not lake—never far away. Though this is indeed the Baker Lake Trail, you won't actually see the lake for a couple miles yet. Expect mud and a few overgrown stretches.

At about **1.2** miles, find yourself on a minor rock outcropping at river's edge with super views of the river, its extensive network of gravel bars (always open), and the surrounding hills. Return to the forest and in a little less than a mile begin what appears to be a climb. Yes, it is a climb, there's even a switchback or two to prove it. Via a bridge, cross Hidden Creek. Given that it's really rushing, really roaring, and really icy, it must be named "Hidden" in the same way that exceedingly tall people are sometimes nicknamed Shorty. Hidden Creek makes a good turnaround point for those inclined to a hike of more like 4 miles round-trip.

The trail continues up and down, becoming a bit more rugged and overgrown at times. The trees—big ol' cedars and Doug firs—become more and more massive and appear to be the legs of giants. At about **3.0** miles, Baker Lake—semi-obscured through the trees—comes into view for the first time. Depending on the lake level, look for tree stumps emerging from lakebed, from when the Baker River was dammed to flood this valley, thus creating Baker Lake. Look for emerging views of Mounts Baker and Shuksan too.

After another not-too-terrible climb, find yourself looking almost straight down at the lake, about 100 feet below. At **4.5** miles, after a gentle descent and bend to the left through an odd, thinned-out, almost boglike stretch, find yourself at the signed Noisy Creek Hiker Camp, your destination. Continue on the trail for about 100 yards to enjoy the cool, stunning water show put on by the so-named creek, which isn't actually all that noisy. Return to the camp sign and go left for about 50 yards through said camping area, right on the lake. Take off your shoes and stick your feet in under the gaze of Baker and Shuksan.

Going Farther

An option before heading back is to explore the obscure trail directly opposite the short trail to Noisy Creek Hiker Camp. This trail, which

PERMITS/CONTACT
Northwest Forest Pass required/Mount Baker–Snoqualmie National Forest, (360) 856-5700

MAPS
USGS Mount Shuksan, Bacon Peak; Green Trails Lake Shannon 46, Mount Shuksan 14

TRAIL NOTES
Leashed dogs okay; kid-friendly; great views

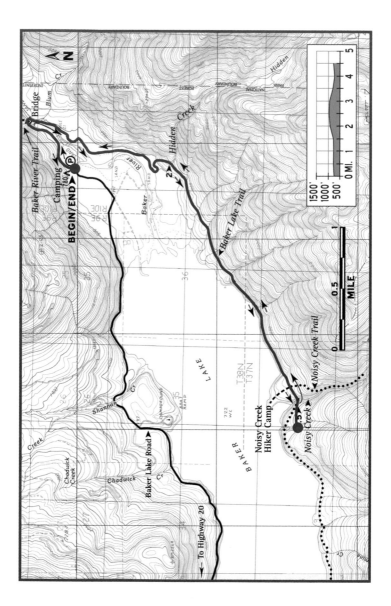

climbs about 700 feet in a mile, leads to a protected old-growth forest and views down into the Noisy Creek gorge.

Also, Baker Lake Trail continues south for about 9.5 more miles to the Baker Lake Trail south trailhead on Baker Dam Road. Total distance from end to end is 14 miles.

Camping is available at the trailhead, at Noisy Creek Hiker Camp, and at several camps along both sides of Baker Lake. ■

7. Sauk Mountain

RATING ★★★ ☆ ☆	DISTANCE 4.2 miles round-trip	HIKING TIME 2 hours
ELEVATION GAIN 1,200 feet	HIGH POINT 5,500 feet	DIFFICULTY ♦♦ ◆ ◆ ◆
BEST SEASON Jan Feb Mar Apr May Jun **Jul Aug Sep Oct** Nov Dec		

The Hike

This south-facing, craggy top is one of the first mountain trails along Highway 20 to be clear of snow and thus usually the first to take you more than a mile high into the sky. Views are splendiferous—from Mounts Baker and Shuksan to the heart of the North Cascades to even Mount Rainier and the Olympics. Because of this trail's easy access and easy grade, crowds are populous here. There's no real forest to speak of; it's strictly a hike for mountain and river lovers.

Getting There

Head east on Highway 20 (North Cascades Highway) to milepost 96, about 7 miles east of Concrete. Turn left on Sauk Mountain Road (Forest Road 1030), across from the milepost. Follow (and climb) for nearly 8 miles. At a fork at about 7.5 miles, bear right; the road-end parking lot is just ahead at 7.7 miles. Elevation: 4,350 feet.

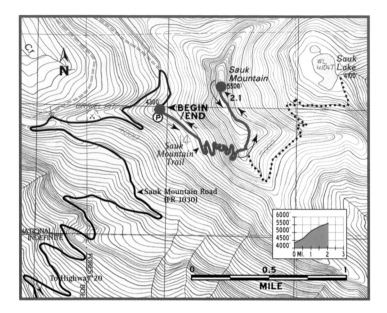

The Trail

After tearing yourself away from the parking-lot views, which are awesome in their own right, dip down briefly and then head up the obvious trail. Then . . . ready, set, switchback! Wind back and forth up an open, south-facing meadow that, depending on the month, offers a festive wildflower show. Look up at the folks who are where you

PERMITS/CONTACT
Northwest Forest Pass required/Mount Baker–Snoqualmie National Forest, (360) 856-5700

MAPS
USGS Sauk Mountain; Green Trails Lake Shannon 46

TRAIL NOTES
Leashed dogs okay; kid-friendly; great views

Sauk Mountain's craggy top

want to be (and are looking down at you), and down at those following in your footsteps (and who are looking up at you). Views south are of mountains, foothills, and multiple river valleys—the Sauk and Skagit meet below your toes for a grand summit. It's an eagle-eye view of the Skagit River Bald Eagle Natural Area, where, in winters, more than 400 eagles come to roost. Sauk Mountain's impressive craggy cockscomb—visible from Interstate 5 and thus a nice gauge for checking the snow level   is directly overhead.

At about **0.4** mile, enter the first stand of trees at a switchback elbow. At about **0.41** mile, exit that stand. Watch for marmots and marmot holes right on the trail; they don't mind crunching an ankle or two. Then switchback a whole lot more, enjoying the increasingly righteous views and the occasional shadelike spot.

At about **1.4** miles, round a bend on the mountain's shoulder and be wowed as the already great views multiply in greatness. The North Cascades' sea of peaks dominates the east, Glacier Peak and her cronies are south, and almost directly below you, the Sauk and the Skagit are getting together for a river dance. Just ahead, a spur trail to the right—sometimes, but not always, signed—leads down to Sauk Lake; stay left.

On the main trail, continue along the ridge crest for about 0.5 mile to a saddle just east of the rocky pinnacles. Northern views come into play, including Mount Shuksan and peaks north of the border. Mount Baker stands to be counted too. Continue along, oohing and aahing at the views, until the trail eventually peters out. Return the same way.

Going Farther

If you've got some time, the 1.5-mile side trip down 1,200 feet to Sauk Lake is worth it, though the trail can be muddy and sketchy in spots.

Camping is available at Rockport State Park, on Highway 20 just east of Sauk Mountain Road. ■

CASCADE PASS

8. Lookout Mountain Trail (near Marblemount)

RATING	DISTANCE	HIKING TIME
★★★★☆	9.4 miles round-trip	6 hours

ELEVATION GAIN	HIGH POINT	DIFFICULTY
4,450 feet	5,699 feet	◆◆◆◆◆

BEST SEASON
Jan Feb Mar Apr May Jun **Jul Aug Sep Oct** Nov Dec

The Hike

This one requires some work in the form of 4,500 feet worth of climbing. But if you love mountaintop vistas and you're a fire lookout buff, definitely put this one on your list. The lookout structure, though no longer used to spot fires, was built in 1962 and is still maintained by a local hiking club.

Getting There

Head east on Highway 20 (North Cascades Highway) to Marblemount, about 40 miles east of Sedro-Woolley. Just past milepost 106, turn right onto Cascade River Road and follow for about 7 miles to a small pullout parking area on the right. The trailhead is across the road. Elevation: 1,300 feet.

PERMITS/CONTACT
Northwest Forest Pass required/Mount Baker–Snoqualmie National Forest, (360) 856-5700

MAPS
USGS Big Devil Peak; Green Trails Marblemount 47

TRAIL NOTES
Leashed dogs okay; deep-in-the-heart-of-the-North Cascades views; extremely steep

---

The fire lookout atop Lookout Mountain affords views of Mounts Baker and Shuksan and the Pickett Range

The Trail

What exactly is the recommended daily allowance of steep switchbacks? I suppose it's a personal preference, but I do know that the first 2.5 miles of the Lookout Mountain Trail pushes whatever your individual inclination is to its limit. The switchbacks are relentless, nonstop, and seemingly never-ending—all in dense forest, too. But that's the price you pay for an easy-access trail that requires no sketchy mountain roads to negotiate. It starts low, just a tad higher than the Cascade River, but in just about 4 miles, places you 4,500 feet above it, where it's nothing but Cascade peaks, ridges, and glaciers as far as the eye can see.

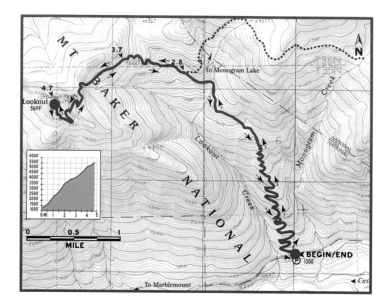

Once on the trail, start climbing (lots) and at **2.8** miles—not far from where the switchbacks peter out, yet the trail continues climbing—reach a signed intersection with the Monogram Lake Trail. Follow the sign for Lookout Mountain. At **3.7** miles, after another switchback stretch, the trail breaks out of the forest and into some open meadows affording spectacular mountain views to the Cascade River valley and beyond.

Among the numerous peaks, ridgelines, and forested folds are Teebone Ridge, Eldorado Peak, Johannesburg Mountain, Hidden Lake Lookout, Snowking Mountain, and so many more. And just above, perched at the edge of a rocky outcrop, is the lookout: a 14-by-14-foot glass box atop a 30-foot tower. Continue climbing, more gradually and buoyed by the mostly open mountain scenery the rest of the way—not to mention mountain blueberries if you time it right—and at **4.7** miles, reach the lookout.

Views extend far in all directions and include everything from Mounts Baker and Shuksan; the Picket Range; the peaks Little Devil,

Eldorado, and Glacier; and lots, lots more. Though not used to spot fires anymore, the lookout itself is maintained by a local hiking group and is available for overnight stays on a first-come basis. Built in 1962, the cabin sports a couple of beds, a gas stove, table and chairs, eating utensils, stuffed animals (three bears, a bunny, and an owl when I was there last) along with a few books to while away the hours.

After you've had your fill, return the same way, being careful on the trail's steep descent. Trekking poles are highly recommended for this trail.

Going Farther
The Monogram Lake Trail leads 2.1 miles to Monogram Lake, climbing 1,200 feet and descending 600 feet along the way. Hidden Lake Lookout access is off FR 1540, about 3 miles farther along Cascade River Road; Boston Basin (Hike 10) is about 15.5 miles farther on Cascade River Road; and Cascade Pass-Sahale Arm (Hike 11) is about 16 miles farther.

Camping is available in the lookout, just below it, and at Marble Creek Campground, about a mile east of the trailhead on Cascade River Road. ∎

9. Hidden Lake Lookout

RATING	DISTANCE	HIKING TIME
★★★★★	9 miles round-trip	6 hours

ELEVATION GAIN	HIGH POINT	DIFFICULTY
3,400 feet	6,890 feet	◆◆◆◆◇

BEST SEASON
Jan Feb Mar Apr May Jun **Jul Aug Sep Oct** Nov Dec

The Hike

This one has it all—a short forest climb, wildflower meadows guarded by sky-kissing rock spires, a scramble-fun summit pyramid crowned with a historic lookout. And, oh yes, a picture-perfect alpine lake. Mountain views galore—Eldorado Peak, Boston Basin, and that whole crowd, not to mention volcanoes from Mount Baker to Glacier Peak to Mount Rainier. The Olympics too. Yum-yum.

Getting There

Head east on Highway 20 (North Cascades Highway) to Marblemount, about 40 miles east of Sedro-Woolley. Just past milepost 106, turn right onto Cascade River Road and follow it for about 9.8 miles (7 of them paved) to Forest Road 1540. Turn left and follow the rough, narrow dirt road for 4.7 miles to the road-end trailhead. Elevation: 3,500 feet.

PERMITS/CONTACT
Northwest Forest Pass required/Mount Baker–Snoqualmie National Forest, (360) 856-5700

MAPS
USGS Eldorado Peak, Sonny Boy Lakes; Green Trails Diablo Dam 48, Cascade Pass 80

TRAIL NOTES
Leashed dogs okay to national park boundary; great views

Lookout views of Eldorado Peak and Hidden Lake

The Trail

At first the trail follows an old roadbed—a rather rocky one at that. Cross several creeks and, soon enough, enter a dark forest of silver firs where the trail meanders while it climbs. A number of wooden bridges and steps keep you off the wet and mushy sections.

At about **1.0** mile, bust out of the forest and enter the open meadow of the Sibley Creek valley. Climb steeply up and across this grand amphitheater of wildflowers, waterfalls, and craggy peaks—the Hidden Lake Peaks, which loom at the head of the basin like something in a Dr. Seuss book. Almost all of this is in the open, thus the climb doesn't seem nearly as strenuous—mountain euphoria eases the grade. Views of Mount Baker and Twin Sisters emerge when switchbacks swing you west.

At about **2.4** miles, the trail takes a turn toward the south and the grade lessens dramatically. Cross a huge heathery and bouldery meadow, a-bustin' with blueberries. Climb some as you cross boulder fields, talusy side slopes, and, more than likely, snow. Avert your

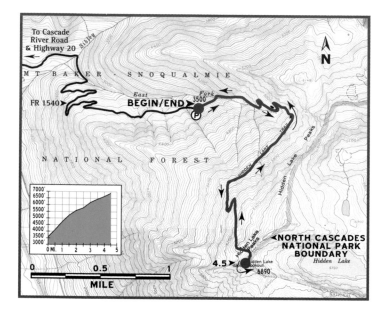

eyes from the nasty clearcuts on the hills across the Cascade River to the west.

The rocky ridge to your left coyly hides views to the east, but in not too much longer you'll be more than rewarded for your patience. At **3.7** miles, things can get tricky and, if there's lots of snow obscuring the trail, downright dangerous. (An ice ax is a requirement for early-season attempts.) Scramble through boulders to attain a minor ridge and gain your first glimpse of the lookout, which looks like something bolted onto a stack of boulders. That's because it is.

(Here's a bonus tip: Whenever you're on a trail that features a lookout, make sure you spot it first so that you can shout "Look out!" hopefully to the heart-stopping annoyance of others in your party.)

At **4.2** miles reach a notch and, just beyond, enter North Cascades National Park. Views east are finally yours. You've found Hidden Lake, not to mention Eldorado, Boston, Forbidden, Sahale, and about a million other peaks, valleys, forests, and rivers. To reach

Quien Sabe Glacier and Boston Basin

the lookout, which is 300 feet above you, go right (south), bearing to the left of the pyramid ridge ahead of you. Look for fading red dots spray-painted on rocks that point the way.

From the lookout, views are even more stupendous—a 360-degree IMAX-esque panorama of the Twin Sisters, Mounts Baker and Shuksan, seemingly every geologic formation in North Cascades National Park, Glacier Peak, Mount Rainier. Goodies galore. The lookout, built in 1931, is maintained by a local volunteer group and is available for camping on a first-come, first-served basis. When I visited here one September morning, I inadvertently crashed a summit party being thrown by about a half dozen ptarmigan.

Going Farther

To reach Hidden Lake, descend the talus slope east of the lookout pyramid. Follow cairns or boot tracks, or find your own way down.

From the notch just below the last pitch to the lookout, it's also possible to head left (north) to scramble up to the top of the nearest Hidden Lakes Peak, which is about 200 feet higher than the lookout. Follow cairns or boot track.

Camping is available at Marble Creek Campground on Cascade River Road, about 3 miles west of the intersection with FR 1540. ∎

10. Boston Basin

RATING	DISTANCE	HIKING TIME
★ ★ ★ ★ ☆	8 miles round-trip	6 hours
ELEVATION GAIN	**HIGH POINT**	**DIFFICULTY**
3,200 feet	6,400 feet	◆ ◆ ◆ ◆ ◆

BEST SEASON											
Jan	Feb	Mar	Apr	May	Jun	**Jul**	**Aug**	**Sep**	**Oct**	Nov	Dec

The Hike

Climbers' trails are horses of a different hue. Their goal is to get you into climbing country as quickly as possible, so don't expect contemplative strolls through forest. However, as this rugged route to Boston Basin proves, some climbers' trails offer day hikers views that are simply out of this world.

Getting There

Head east on Highway 20 (North Cascades Highway) to Marblemount, about 40 miles east of Sedro-Woolley. Just past milepost 106, turn right onto Cascade River Road and follow it for 22.5 miles, the last 16 on gravel, to a small parking area on your left. (If this lot is full, park at the Cascade Pass trailhead parking lot about 0.5 mile farther, at the end of Cascade River Road.) Elevation: 3,200 feet.

The Trail

Though this trail is often overgrown and easy to miss, an old trailhead kiosk with map will assure you that you've got the right place. The trail starts by following an old miners' road for about a mile. (If you're using the USGS map, the beginning of the trail is shown as an old road to a diamond mine.) Behind you, grand and glorious Johannesburg Mountain roars its thunderhead roar, releasing avalanches into the Cascade River valley, seemingly by the dozen. Rumbling at all hours, this is the kind of mountain that shoots all to heck the rule of thumb that avalanches occur only after noon.

At about **1.0** mile, huge views of Boston Basin open to the north and of the Hidden Lake Peaks area to the west. Now the fun begins. The trail narrows, steepens, and becomes a primitive, overgrown boot path that requires hands as well as feet on some stretches. Thankfully, it's not exposed; otherwise we'd be talking about ropes here. After a few hundred yards, the trail returns to semi-normal, though it remains steep.

Continue climbing steadily through forest, crossing a number of creeks (the number varies according to meltwater level), most without bridges and several being fairly tricky—trekking poles or a walking stick are highly recommended, if not required. At about **3.0** miles emerge from the forest and enter the open lower reaches of Boston Basin—truly spectacular. Your personal mountain IMAX vision includes Mount Torment and Forbidden Peak to the north and Boston Peak and Sahale Mountain to the east, with their huge, shared Quien Sabe Glacier stealing all focus. A couple of big creeks remain to be crossed, and not too much farther, the snow level will dictate how far you can go.

The trail continues up a hogsback of a moraine—marmot central—and forks at about **4.0** miles. To the left, reach a talus-strewn camp area in about 0.25 mile where you'll find great full-on, eye-to-eye views of Johannesburg Mountain, Cascade Peak, and the Triplets. Continuing straight at the fork, the trail eventually peters out, but one can follow boot track through loose rock to the foot of the Quien Sabe Glacier. The huge, flat slabs of rock have been scoured so

---

PERMITS/CONTACT
Northwest Forest Pass required/North Cascades National Park, Marblemount Ranger Station, (360) 873-4590

MAPS
USGS Cascade Pass (trail not shown); Green Trails Cascade Pass 80 (trail not shown)

TRAIL NOTES
No dogs; great views

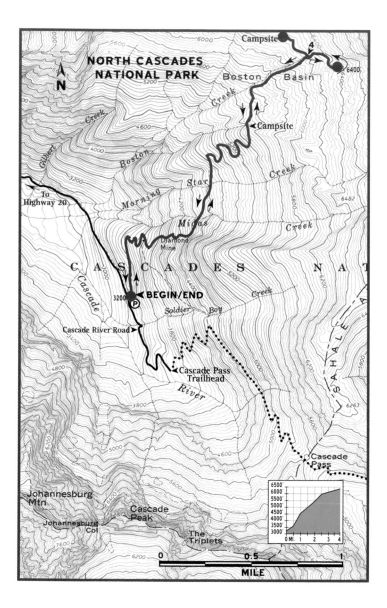

NORTH CASCADES
NATIONAL PARK

N

Campsite

4

6400'

Boston   Basin

Creek

To
Highway 20

Gilbert   Creek

Boston

Morning   Star

Midas

Diamond
Mine

Campsite

Creek

6482

Creek

N   A   T

CASCADES

Cascade

3200'

P   BEGIN/END

Soldier   Boy

Creek

6200'

SAHALE

Cascade River Road

River

Cascade Pass
Trailhead

Cascade
Pass

6263

Johannesburg
Mtn.

Johannesburg
Col

Cascade
Peak

The
Triplets

6500'
6000'
5500'
5000'
4500'
4000'
3500'
3000'
0 Mi. 1 2 3 4

0   0.5   1
MILE

smooth by the receding glacier that they're banana-peel slippery, so watch your step. Do as they do in Italy and roam.

Going Farther

The Cascade Pass–Sahale Arm Trail (Hike 11) is just 0.5 mile farther up Cascade River Road.

Camping is available at various campgrounds on Cascade River Road, such as Mineral Park, about 5 miles before the trailhead. ∎

11. Cascade Pass–Sahale Arm

RATING	DISTANCE	HIKING TIME
★★★★★	7.4 to 12.4 miles round-trip	0 hours
ELEVATION GAIN	**HIGH POINT**	**DIFFICULTY**
1,800 to 3,500 feet	7,000 feet	◆◆◆◆

BEST SEASON
Jan Feb Mar Apr May Jun **Jul Aug Sep Oct** Nov Dec

The Hike

Popular and oft populated, Cascade Pass's abundance of peaks, glaciers, meadows, and waterfalls—all accessible with relative ease—makes it a true crowd pleaser. The parking-lot view of Johannesburg Mountain is enough to spike the mountain mojo of most folks, and the views are only better at the pass. If crowds give you the willies, head for nearby Boston Basin (Hike 10) or Hidden Lake Lookout (Hike 9).

Getting There

Head east on Highway 20 (North Cascades Highway) to Marblemount, about 40 miles east of Sedro Woolley. Just past milepost 106, turn right onto Cascade River Road and follow it for about 23 miles, the last 17 on gravel, to the road-end parking lot. Elevation: 3,600 feet.

Running fast above Cascade Pass

The Trail

Once you're able to tear yourself away from the views of Johannesburg Mountain's spectacular hanging glaciers, shimmering waterfalls, rocky spires, and craggy folds, find the trailhead at the opposite end of the parking lot. The wide trail begins by switchbacking gently through forest. Soon enough the grade steepens and finally, at about **2.5** miles, leaves the timberland and emerges into open meadows. (You might lose sight of Johannesburg from time to

PERMITS/CONTACT
Northwest Forest Pass required/North Cascades National Park,
Marblemount Ranger Station, (360) 873-4500

MAPS
USGS Cascade Pass; Green Trails Cascade Pass 80

TRAIL NOTES
No dogs; great views

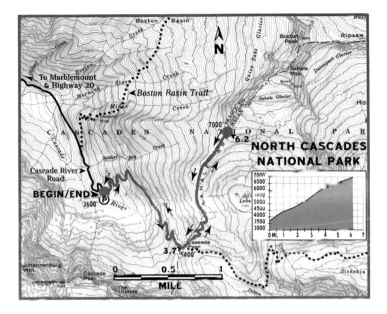

time, but you'll almost always hear it—avalanches crash down the mountain at all hours of the day and night. Luckily, the massif is across the Cascade River valley, so hikers are not in danger of avalanches from that peak.) Mountain views return, now exponentially increased, and you'll swear that you're hiking in the clouds. Cascade Peak, the Triplets, and to the southeast Magic Mountain now join Johannesburg in this high-country mountain party.

From here it's mostly a gentle traverse through meadow and across talus slope, with one bump to hump just before you reach Cascade Pass at **3.7** miles. Views east from the pass into the Stehekin River valley are truly spectacular; if you're not up for going any farther, this meadowy saddle is a great place to turn around.

If you are going farther, and higher, follow the sign to the left (north) for Sahale Arm and begin an extremely steep, rocky climb that gains about 700 feet in 0.75 mile. At **4.4** miles, crest a ridge and be amazed while you gaze at Sahale Mountain's rocky, glacier-draped summit pyramid, kind of like a mini (but not too mini) Mount Shuksan. Far below, some 800 feet, sits Doubtful Lake, like a giant emerald stuck in a hole at the bottom of a basin.

Continue up and to the left, following the meadows of Sahale Arm as far as the snow level allows. Somehow, views become even more incredible as Forbidden Peak, Mount Torment, and Eldorado Peak enter the picture. Reach Sahale Glacier at **6.2** miles, a great turnaround spot for those without ropes, ice axes, and glacier travel experience.

Going Farther

The trail to Boston Basin (Hike 10) is 0.5 mile down Cascade River Road from this trailhead.

At Cascade Pass, the trail continues east toward Stehekin.

Camping is allowed near the trailhead and at the edge of Sahale Glacier, as well as at various campgrounds on Cascade River Road, such as Mineral Park, about 5 miles before the trailhead. ■

DIABLO AND ROSS LAKES

12. Thornton Lakes–Trappers Peak

RATING	DISTANCE	HIKING TIME
★★★★★	10.2 to 11.8 miles round-trip	7 hours
ELEVATION GAIN	**HIGH POINT**	**DIFFICULTY**
2,550 to 3,400 feet	5,964 feet	◆◆◆◆◇

BEST SEASON
Jan Feb Mar Apr May Jun **Jul Aug Sep Oct** Nov Dec

The Hike

With names that fit their rep—Mount Terror, Mount Fury—the Pickets are perhaps the most rugged mountain range in the North Cascades. Trappers Peak offers gigantic Picket peaks—and dozens of other peaks—as well as way-down views to the snaking Skagit River and the sleepy burg of Newhalem, gateway to Diablo.

Getting There

Head east on Highway 20 (North Cascades Highway) to milepost 117.3, about 11 miles east of Marblemount, and turn left onto Thornton Lakes Road. Follow the rough gravel road for about 5.1 miles to the road-end trailhead. Elevation: 2,700 feet.

The Trail

Start out by loosening up those quads 'n' calves on the first 2 miles of this forest trail, which follows an old roadbed and, as such, gains elevation very gradually. Still roadwide in spots, the trail crosses

---

PERMITS/CONTACT
Northwest Forest Pass required/North Cascades National Park, North Cascades Visitor Center, (360) 854-7200

MAPS
USGS Mount Triumph; Green Trails Marblemount 47

TRAIL NOTES
No dogs; great views

Thorton Lakes below Mount Triumph

several creeks and offers occasional glimpses north to the ridge above Thornton Lakes, your eventual destination.

At about **2.3** miles, round a bend and begin climbing in earnest on a more typical North Cascades trail, which means no more road-wide stretches. Ascend through hemlock forest for a little more than a mile, crossing the odd muddy spot, and reach a small open mead-owy area just before entering North Cascades National Park. Climb steeply for another mile and at **4.5** miles, shortly after having broken through the trees and been treated to hints of the mega-mountain views that await you above, reach a signed intersection with the trail down to the Thornton Lakes.

For Thornton Lakes: To reach the first—and largest—of the Thornton Lakes, go left and drop about 600 feet over the next 0.6 mile. The two others, located beyond the first lake, require more dif-ficult cross-country travel to get to. Return the same way.

For Trappers Peak: To continue on about 0.8 mile to Trappers Peak, at the intersection go straight and start climbing seemingly straight up via a primitive but easy-to-follow trail. In a couple hun-dred yards, reach a notch that affords stunning views down to the

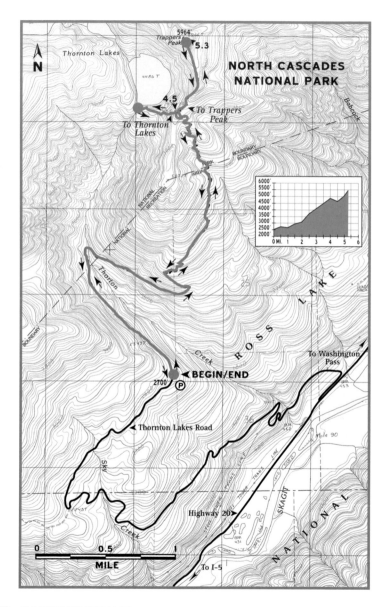

N

Thornton Lakes

NORTH CASCADES
NATIONAL PARK

5964'
Trappers
Peak **5.3**

4486 T

4.5

*To Trappers
Peak*

*To Thornton
Lakes*

Babcock

6000'
5500'
5000'
4500'
4000'
3500'
3000'
2500'
2000'
0 Mi. 1 2 3 4 5 6

Thornton

R O S S   L A K E

To Washington
Pass

Creek

2700' **BEGIN/END**
Ⓟ

◄ Thornton Lakes Road

Sky

Highway 20 ►

SKAGIT   CREEK

Mile 90

N A T I O N A L

Creek

0   0.5   1

MILE

To I-5

The Picket Range from Trappers Peak

jewel-like Thornton Lakes sitting peacefully in the lap of glaciated Mount Triumph. If you're about whupped, this makes a fine turn-around point, at about **4.6** miles. If you're up for more, scramble on following the rough trail to the right.

Soon reach a couple of full-on scramble stretches where you're using your hands as well as your feet to proceed. (It's not exposed, so it's not as scary as it seems at first.) You'll pop completely out of the trees and find yourself surrounded on all sides by mountain, valley, and river views. The most immediate mountain is directly north—Trappers Peak—the top of which is where you'll find yourself in about 20 minutes, after a challenging, but not impossible, steep hike up its spine.

From the bouldery summit of Trappers Peak, the 360-degree views are major jaw-droppers. You've got your lakes, your Pickets to the north, your Teebone Ridge and Eldorado Peak to the south, your Colonial Peak massif to the east, and your on-and-on views forever and ever. This vista is why they put that little panoramic button on your camera. Return the same way.

Going Farther
Camping is available at Goodell Creek and Newhalem Campgrounds, about 3 miles east of Thornton Lakes Road on Highway 20. ∎

13. Skagit River Loop

RATING	DISTANCE	HIKING TIME
★★ ☆ ☆ ☆	1.8-mile loop	1 hour
ELEVATION GAIN	**HIGH POINT**	**DIFFICULTY**
100 feet	570 feet	♦ ◇ ◇ ◇ ◇

BEST SEASON
Jan Feb Mar Apr May Jun Jul Aug Sep Oct Nov Dec

The Hike

In not much distance, this gentle, rainy-day walk offers myriad pleasant surprises. Pass through several phases of forest—from post-burn to old growth to post-logged—and rock-hop in the shallows of one of the Northwest's great rivers. Another plus: This loop is wheelchair accessible.

Getting There

Head east on Highway 20 (North Cascades Highway) to milepost 120 and the North Cascades National Park Visitors Center in Newhalem, about 53 miles east of Sedro-Woolley. Turn right and continue about a mile, past Newhalem Campground, to the visitors center. The trailhead is just behind the building, on the right. Elevation: 570 feet.

Note: You can start at Newhalem Creek Campground to avoid the one big hill back up to the visitors center, and to shorten the hike by 0.8 mile. The well-signed campground is on the right, about 0.25 mile before the visitors center. Go to the west end of the campground road to find the loop trail. Elevation: 500 feet.

The Trail

After checking out the interpretive sign at the visitors center trailhead to read about what you're likely to see, head down the long, gentle slope into the forested valley. Listen for the not-too-far-off rumble of the Skagit River. On the valley floor, pass through post-burn stands of pine and listen for the crackle of fires—campfires, that is. At about **0.4** mile, Loops A and B of the Newhalem Creek Campground are

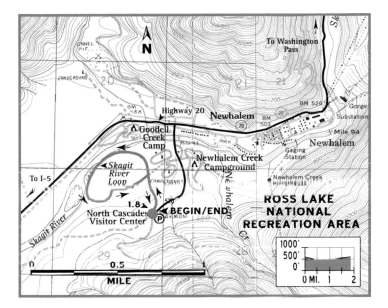

just to the right; the return loop is to the left—go straight. (All trail intersections are well-marked: Follow signs for River Loop Trail on the way to the river, and signs for Visitors Center on the way back.)

At about **0.7** mile, after rounding a bend, suddenly find yourself in a dense old stand of massive cedars and firs, and their attendant mosses, lichens, and ferns—the whole rain-forest gang present and accounted for. In a couple hundred yards you'll spot the mighty

PERMITS/CONTACT
Northwest Forest Pass required/North Cascades Visitor Center,
(360) 854-7200

MAPS
USGS Mount Triumph; Green Trails Marblemount 47

TRAIL NOTES
Leashed dogs okay; kid-friendly; wheelchair accessible

Misty hills above the Skagit River

Skagit River through the trees. Just ahead, find several river access points from which you can get some face time with the river. (And get wet feet, if so inclined.) In fall and winter, be careful; salmon spawn here in the shallows. Look for American dippers, curtsey-happy birds that make like submarines and cruise stream bottoms for insects. Look up for views of Trappers Peak (Hike 12) across the river.

Back on the trail, continue paralleling the river for a few hundred yards. Soon enter a deciduous forest, followed by a return to pine-heavy woods. At **1.4** miles, reach the intersection that you came to earlier. This time, go right, following the sign for the visitors center. From here, return the same way you came.

Going Farther

Camping is available at the Newhalem Creek Campground, located in the same visitors center complex, and at Goodell Creek Campground, just outside the complex on Highway 20. ■

14. Sourdough Mountain Trail

RATING	DISTANCE	HIKING TIME
★★★★ ☆	11.4 miles round-trip	9 hours

ELEVATION GAIN	HIGH POINT	DIFFICULTY
5,100 feet	5,985 feet	♦ ♦ ♦ ♦ ♦

BEST SEASON
Jan Feb Mar Apr May **Jun Jul Aug Sep Oct** Nov Dec

The Hike

There are trails that claim to be Mother Nature's Thighmaster—and then there's Sourdough Mountain. Gain roughly 1,000 feet per mile for 5-plus miles, but not without remuneration. Views from Sourdough Mountain's lookout—built in 1933 at one of the first fire lookout sites in the nation—are 360-degree, top-of-the-world head spinners. Mountains, glaciers, and two amazing lakes—Ross and Diablo.

Getting There

Head east on Highway 20 (North Cascades Highway) to milepost 126, about 6 miles east of Newhalem, and turn left onto Diablo Road. Follow it for about a mile and park at the pullout area on the right. The trailhead sign is across the street about 50 yards, next to a bubble-topped swimming pool. The trail starts about 50 feet to the right of the sign behind the pool. Elevation: 900 feet.

PERMITS/CONTACT
Northwest Forest Pass required/North Cascades Visitor Center,
(360) 854-7200

MAPS
USGS Diablo Dam, Ross Dam, Pumpkin Mountain;
Green Trails Diablo Dam 48, Ross Lake 16

TRAIL NOTES
No dogs; great views

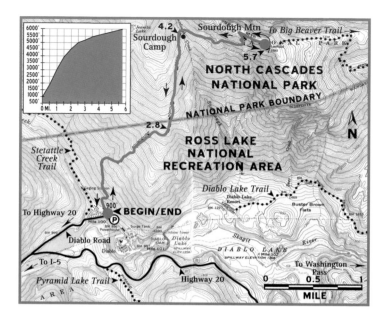

The Trail

Ready. Set. Climb. And steeply at that. First through a small boulder field, then through forest. Then trees. Then woods. Occasional breaks in those mostly green-leafed and/or needled, woody plants reveal glimpses of the Colonial Peak massif and Gorge Lake to the south, and the Stetattle Creek drainage to the west, all of which you'll see in much greater glory. But not for a while. In the meantime, climb. Through forest. Trees. And woods.

At about **2.5** miles, after you've climbed about 3,000 feet, the grade lessens for a bit, the trees part a tad, and you're treated to some great southern views—Colonial and Pyramid Peaks and their attendant glaciers and waterfalls. Resume climbing, now a little less steeply and in forest with openings that allow more peeks to surrounding peaks. At about **2.8** miles enter North Cascades National Park.

The trail narrows as it traverses a fold in the mountain, allowing views down to turquoise tinted Diablo Lake. (The color is from glacial sediments deposited in the lake by Thunder Creek. The sediments are so fine they remain suspended in the water instead of settling at the bottom. Because it's not fed by Thunder Creek, nearby Ross Lake is not the same shade of green, as you'll see when you reach the lookout.) Straight ahead (and up) you can see a 1,500-foot wall of meadow topped by a fairly level ridge—that's your destination.

At **4.2** miles, reach Sourdough Creek and Sourdough Camp, a great place to fill up on (and filter) some water, and recharge for the final 1,000-foot, 1.5-mile push to the top. Of course, you might not need it. This last stretch is almost entirely in open, wildflower meadows and the views are simply glorious—more Cascades, glaciers, valleys, and waterfalls than you can shake a dozen sticks at. Diablo Lake, almost a mile below you now, dominates all and is a serious eyeball magnet of a lake if there ever was one.

Views double in transplendence when you reach the ridge in about a mile. The Pickets and Elephant Butte to the northwest, Jack Mountain to the east, Hozomeen Mountain to the northeast as well as Ross Lake and the dozens of named and unnamed peaks along its shores are all here—serious mountain overload danger, this one. Head to the right along the ridge and reach the working lookout in about 0.5 mile. Same great views, only even better, if that's possible. Eat, drink, hitch a ride from gravity on the way back down.

Going Farther

For a less steep but longer hike up Sourdough Mountain, follow the Ross Dam Trail (Hike 19) across the dam and pick up the Big Beaver Trail, which follows Ross Lake's west shore. Continue for about 3 fairly level miles until the trail intersects with the Sourdough Mountain Trail. Go left and climb about 4,000 feet over the next 5.5 miles to the lookout, following cairns for about the last mile.

Also in the vicinity are the Diablo Lake Trail (Hike 16) and the Pyramid Lake Trail (Hike 15).

Camping is available along Highway 20 at Goodell Creek and Newhalem Campgrounds to the west and at Colonial Creek Campground to the east. ■

15. Pyramid Lake Trail

RATING	DISTANCE	HIKING TIME
★ ★ ★ ☆ ☆	4.2 miles round-trip	2 hours
ELEVATION GAIN	**HIGH POINT**	**DIFFICULTY**
1,550 feet	2,600 feet	♦ ♦ ◇ ◇ ◇
	BEST SEASON	
	Jan Feb Mar Apr May Jun Jul Aug Sep Oct Nov Dec	

The Hike

Short but fairly steep, Pyramid Lake Trail offers an excellent early-season wilderness experience in microcosm. Climb steadily through post-burn pines, pass through a cool creek valley inhabited by 500-year-old cedars, and finally ponder the pond that is deep, dark Pyramid Lake. Topping out at about 2,600 feet, this hike is a good one for working up a shoulder-season sweat.

Getting There

Head east on Highway 20 (North Cascades Highway) to about milepost 126.7, about 7 miles east of Newhalem. The roadside parking area is on the left (north) side of the road just after a sharp bend in the highway. The signed trailhead is on the opposite side of the road. Elevation: 1,100 feet.

The Trail

Carefully cross Highway 20, and after finding the obvious trailhead by gushing Pyramid Creek, begin climbing immediately. The narrow trail tends toward the rocky, so be careful with your footing, especially later on the way down. Climb steadily through a forest of lodgepole pine and the occasional fir—successors and survivors of a past forest fire—taking a look around every once in a while to see which peaks you can make out. Behind you, looming through the trees, are Davis Peak to the left and Sourdough Mountain to the right. At **0.7** mile, catch your first glimpse of 7,182-foot Pyramid Peak, as aptly named as a mountain can be.

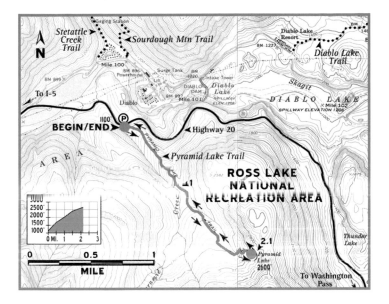

About 0.25 mile ahead, stop climbing for a stretch and arrive at a cool, damp creek valley where the cedar trees are as old as they are tall. Five hundred years old, some of them, and tall enough that you'll swear someone turned down the sun with a dimmer switch. Cross a branch of Pyramid Creek via some well-placed rocks and after about 100 yards of such loveliness, the trail resumes climbing. Continue in dense forest and after several small creek crossings, begin the final push to the lake at about **1.8** miles.

PERMITS/CONTACT
Northwest Forest Pass required/North Cascades Visitor Center,
(360) 854-7200

MAPS
USGS Diablo Dam; Green Trails Diablo Dam 48

TRAIL NOTES
Leashed dogs okay

Pyramid Peak watches over Pyramid Lake

After a final rocky and root-strewn stretch, reach Pyramid Lake. Scramble down the bouldered bank and to the left for great views of Pyramid Peak. Impressive cliffs reflect in the deep dark lake while skittish water beetles skate across the surface. Great place to eat lunch and look for newts—the rough-skinned variety, that is. They've kind of got the run of the place. Also of Discovery Channel potential: sundew, the insect-eating plant that grows on the lake's many decaying floating logs. When you've had enough, return the same way.

Going Farther

Also in the vicinity are the Sourdough Mountain Trail (Hike 14 and the Diablo Lake Trail (Hike 16).

Camping is available along Highway 20 at Goodell Creek and Newhalem Campgrounds to the west and at Colonial Creek Campground to the east. ■

16. Diablo Lake Trail

RATING	DISTANCE	HIKING TIME
★★★ ☆☆	3.8 to 7.6 miles round-trip	2 hours
ELEVATION GAIN	HIGH POINT	DIFFICULTY
850 feet	2,000 feet	◆ ◆ ◇ ◇ ◇

BEST SEASON
Jan Feb Mar Apr May Jun Jul Aug Sep Oct Nov Dec

The Hike

For a low-elevation shoulder-season hike, this trail does its darnedest to offer a high-elevation mountain experience. Great views to be had both up—to Colonial and Pyramid Peaks—and down—to turquoise Diablo Lake some 700 feet below. Also nice: In summers, this less-than-4-mile trail can be done as a one-way hike by taking advantage of the Diablo Ferry, as described below.

Getting There

Head east on Highway 20 (North Cascades Highway) to about milepost 127.4 and the sign for Diablo Dam Access Road, about 7.5 miles east of Newhalem. Follow the narrow road across the top of Diablo Dam and, once across, turn right. A couple hundred yards ahead on the right, there is parking near the sign for Diablo Lake Ferry if you'll be catching the boat. To reach the west (signed) trailhead, continue about 0.25 mile up the paved road from the ferry parking area. Elevation of both starting points: 1,200 feet.

Pyramid Peak rises high above Diablo Lake

Note: From June to October, the ferry, which is run by Seattle City Light, leaves for Ross Lake at 8:30 a.m. and 3 p.m. Cost is $10. For information, call (206) 386-4393.

The Trail

This trail can be done as a 7.6-mile round-trip starting at the west trailhead, which is just east of the ferry dock. If you decide to hike this trail from the west (whether as a round-trip or a one-way west to east, catching the afternoon ferry back to the starting point), follow the trail description below, in reverse.

Here, this trail description assumes you'll be catching that morning ferry to the eastern trailhead near Ross Dam. After the relaxing

PERMITS/CONTACT
Northwest Forest Pass required/North Cascades Visitor Center,
(360) 854-7200

MAPS
USGS Ross Dam; Green Trails Diablo Dam 48

TRAIL NOTES
Leashed dogs okay; great views

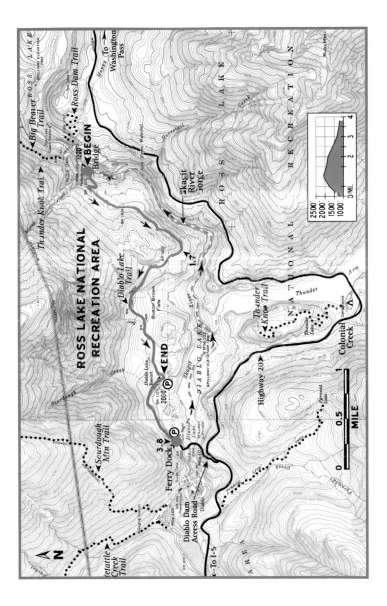

20-minute cruise up the awesome Skagit River Gorge aboard the ferry *Cascadian*, hike a couple yards to a suspension bridge just below Ross Lake Dam. Following the sign for Diablo Lake Trail, cross the bridge and head right. But first, take a moment to ooh and aah over Riprap Creek ripping and rapping its way waterfall-style through cracks in the rock at the base of Sourdough Mountain.

Once across the bridge, begin climbing immediately up a somewhat primitive, not overly maintained trail. Along with the sound of the falls, you'll hear a steady buzz and occasional beeps from a power station by the Ross Lake Dam. Serenity comes later. At **0.3** mile, come to an open power-line area at the edge of a fir forest. Views of Ross Dam emerge behind you, as do the first views of Ruby Mountain to the south. A few hundred yards ahead, a sign points about 150 feet to the right to one of the least-inspiring signed overlooks in the North Cascades. Skip it and continue hiking to the left.

At about **1.0** mile, the trail, though it continues climbing, does so at a much gentler grade. A couple hundred yards ahead, recross the same power-line area you did before, only this time about 500 feet higher. From here, the trail levels off and views improve as the trail traverses a cliff high above the Skagit and where, not long ago, you were leaning out of the *Cascadian* staring wide-eyed up at these rocky cliffs. No handrails, and it's about 800 feet down to the lake, so draw those young ones near.

At **1.7** miles, after crossing a boulder field or two—one of this trail's running themes—Pyramid, Colonial, and Snowfield Peaks reveal themselves in their glacial and snowfield finery to the south. A stunning massif if there ever was one. Below, the otherworldly green of Diablo Lake demands attention too. Diablo Lake is fed by Thunder Creek, which brings a glacial flour of Skagit gneiss to the lake. Rather than settling at the bottom of the lake, the flour stays suspended in the water and turns an emerald green in the sun. Thus the nice (ahem) color. Speaking of color, in summers, wildflowers on the side of this hill are dazzling.

Views continue to improve and after you round a bend, Davis Peak and other hills north of Highway 20 come into view. At **2.0** miles an unsigned trail spur to the left leads about 50 feet to a bench and what would be some spectacular mountain and lake views were it not for the dozen or so power lines right in your line of sight. As it is, it's still a great view.

Back on the main trail, the way reenters forest and starts giving back much of the elevation you gained earlier. Cross a few more boulder fields, a few more creek beds—both wet and dry. I once came upon a large black bear at about **2.4** miles. After trying to scramble up a tree, he moseyed back my way on the trail, then sauntered off into the woods after deciding I was no threat to his existence. At about **3.4** miles, the trail comes to a dirt road. Follow the trail to the right and in just a few hundred yards come to the west trailhead at a paved road, about 0.25 mile from the ferry parking area.

Going Farther
Nearby are the Sourdough Mountain Trail (Hike 14), Pyramid Lake Trail (Hike 15), Ross Dam Trail (Hike 19), and Big Beaver Trail.

Camping is available about 4 miles west on Highway 20 at Colonial Creek Campground. ■

17. Thunder Knob Trail

RATING	DISTANCE	HIKING TIME
★★★ ☆☆	3.8 miles round-trip	2 hours
ELEVATION GAIN	HIGH POINT	DIFFICULTY
650 feet	1,875 feet	◆◆ ◇◇◇
BEST SEASON		
Jan Feb Mar Apr May Jun Jul Aug Sep Oct Nov Dec		

The Hike
This trail surprises with views where you might not have thought any existed. Wide and gently graded, this winding trail through pleasant forest culminates with 360-degree peeks of Pyramid Peak, Diablo Lake, Jack Mountain, Thunder Arm, and more. Benches and interpretive signage provide a place to rest and a chance to learn.

Diablo Lake and Sourdough Mountain from Thunder Knob

Getting There

Head east on Highway 20 (North Cascades Highway) to Colonial Creek Campground, just past milepost 130.3, about 10 miles east of Newhalem. Enter the campground on the north (left) side of the road. To get to the trailhead, follow a series of footbridges that pass several campsites on the way to the trail. Elevation: 1,230 feet.

The Trail

From the trailhead, start by crossing Colonial Creek via a bridge. Soon enter a dense moss- and fern-carpeted forest so lush and green you half expect to round a bend and startle a leprechaun or

PERMITS/CONTACT
Northwest Forest Pass required/North Cascades Visitor Center,
(360) 854-7200

MAPS
USGS Ross Dam (trail not shown); Green Trails Diablo Dam 48 (trail not shown)

TRAIL NOTES
Leashed dogs okay; kid-friendly; wheelchair-accessible (with assistance)

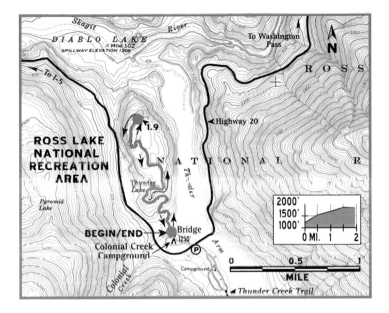

two. Luxuriate in the 3-foot-wide trail that's designated "primitive accessible," meaning that with a little assistance, wheelchair users should be able to access the trail.

After some gentle switchbacks—the grade throughout is never more than 10 percent—views of Colonial Peak and Thunder Arm emerge through the trees. At **1.0** mile reach a semi-open shoulder where more mountain views arrive. From here, with most of the uphill climbing behind you, the trail mostly meanders through forest. At **1.5** miles, a brief switchbacking dip takes you through a boggy area dotted with tiny ponds.

Reach the top in a little less than 0.5 mile, where the trail diverges, offering a couple of different vistas. Head left at the fork and in about 20 yards you're treated with views to the west and north of Pyramid Mountain, Davis Peak, Diablo Lake, and Sourdough Mountain. McMillan Spires is the distant lobster claw reaching for the sky. Continue straight at the fork for about 100 yards to eastern views of Sourdough (that's one big mountain), Jack, and Ruby Mountains. (Jack Mountain and Ruby Mountain—that's odd.) See also the large viewpoint parking lot on Highway 20, a place you've probably stopped yourself—imagine it, people are now down there looking up at you.

Return the same way.

Going Farther

The Thunder Creek–Fourth of July Pass Trail (Hike 18) starts just across the highway from the other side of the campground.

Camping is available at the trailhead at Colonial Creek Campground. ■

18. Thunder Creek–Fourth of July Pass

RATING	DISTANCE	HIKING TIME
★★★☆☆	10.2 miles round-trip	7 hours
ELEVATION GAIN	HIGH POINT	DIFFICULTY
2,600 feet	3,600 feet	◆◆◆◆◇
BEST SEASON		
Jan Feb Mar Apr May Jun Jul Aug Sep Oct Nov Dec		

The Hike

Topping out at just under 3,600 feet, Fourth of July Pass is an early-to-open, late-to-close gem that offers just about everything a lad or lass pines for in a shoulder-season day trip. Meander among monstrous firs and cedars along thunderous Thunder Creek, elevate the heart rate while climbing through stream-streaked woods, enjoy lunch while being wowed by Snowfield Peak and Neve Glacier. This whets one's appetite for summer's higher-elevation hikes.

Peeking through trees at the North Cascades

Getting There

Head east on Highway 20 (North Cascades Highway) to Colonial Creek Campground at milepost 130.3, about 10 miles east of Newhalem. Enter the campground on the south (right) side of the road and follow signs for Thunder Creek trailhead. Elevation: 1,200 feet.

The Trail

After taking a look at the trailhead map, head out past the campground amphitheater along the wide, mostly flat, waterside trail. At **0.2** mile, consider taking a quick side trip on the Thunder Woods

---

PERMITS/CONTACT
Northwest Forest Pass required/North Cascades Visitor Center,
(360) 854-7200

MAPS
USGS Ross Dam; Green Trails Diablo Dam 48

TRAIL NOTES
Leashed dogs okay

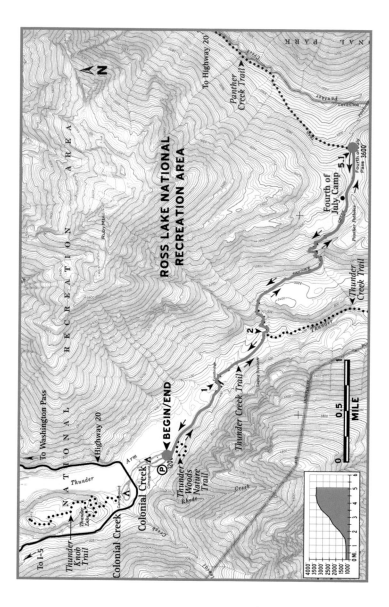

Dam holding back Ross Lake

Nature Trail, a 0.9-mile jaunt through some massive trees. On the main trail, watch through the trees as the emerald waters of Diablo Lake's Thunder Arm narrow and resolve themselves into a rushing stream called Thunder Creek.

At about **1.0** mile, cross Thunder Creek via a cable-stay bridge. Ogle the rushing waters below and look for water ouzels (also called dippers), little blue-gray, sparrow-sized birds that live and dive among the rushing water. Once across, the trail narrows and is given to mud and overgrowth but is nonetheless easy to follow. At **1.8** miles, at the sign for Thunder Creek Camp, continue straight. About 0.25 mile farther, at the trail junction, leave Thunder Creek Trail and go left at the sign for Fourth of July Pass.

Say goodbye to the flatlands, because over the next 2.5 miles, the trail climbs 2,000 feet. It's a forested mix of semi-rocky switchbacks, easy creek crossings, and good old-fashioned steep hiking. Reach Fourth of July Camp at **4.6** miles and bask in the mountain views and sounds. Colonial Peak, Snowfield Peak, and Neve Glacier are striking, the sound of their far-off, booming avalanches awesome.

Continue through a short stretch of dark forest with lots of downed trees to the Panther Potholes—small, dark ponds surrounded by huge cliffs. A large rock to the right of the trail offers a great sit-and-stare spot. Return the same way.

Going Farther

A popular one-way hike is to continue through the Fourth of July Pass and follow the Panther Creek Trail about 6 miles as it descends the Panther Creek valley to the trailhead on Highway 20 at milepost 138.4.

From the Fourth of July Pass trail junction at 2.0 miles, the Thunder Creek Trail continues south more than 30 miles, part of a network of popular backpacking trails. A good day-hike destination is McAllister Creek, about a 12-mile round-trip.

The trailhead for the Thunder Knob Trail (Hike 17) is nearby.

Camping is available at the trailhead at Colonial Creek Campground, on the trail near Fourth of July Pass, and at several camps along the Thunder Creek Trail. ∎

19. Ross Dam

RATING	DISTANCE	HIKING TIME
★★★ ☆☆	**2 miles round-trip**	**1 hour**
ELEVATION GAIN	**HIGH POINT**	**DIFFICULTY**
520 feet	**2,150 feet**	♦ ♦ ◇ ◇ ◇

BEST SEASON
Jan Feb Mar Apr **May Jun Jul Aug Sep Oct** Nov Dec

The Hike

Completed in 1952, Ross Dam raised the level of the Skagit River several hundred feet in order to maintain its level about 20 miles north at the US-Canada border. This trail takes you down to and across the top of the dam and offers dizzying views 500 feet down its spillway.

Getting There

Head east on Highway 20 (North Cascades Highway) to about milepost 134, about 14 miles east of Newhalem. The large trailhead parking lot is on the left (north) side of the road. Elevation: 2,150 feet.

The Trail

Unlike most trails in this book, the destination, the dam, is the trail's low point—in terms of elevation, that is. Start by zigging and zagging down through open pine and fir forest, crossing Happy Creek via a bridge in the first **0.25** mile. Views of Colonial and Pyramid Peaks emerge the lower you go. At about **0.6** mile, pop out of the forest

PERMITS/CONTACT
Northwest Forest Pass required/North Cascades Visitor Center,
(360) 854-7200

MAPS
USGS Ross Dam; Green Trails Mount Diablo Dam 48

TRAIL NOTES
Leashed dogs okay; kid-friendly; great views

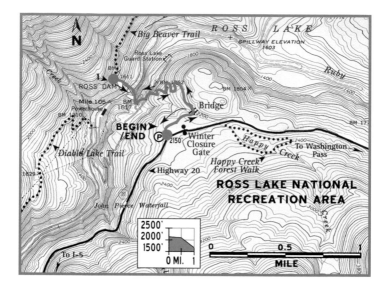

and at a dirt road go left, following the sign for Ross Dam. After a few hundred yards, reach another dirt road. This time go right and reach the dam just ahead at the bottom of the hill.

The top of the dam is about 0.25 mile across and offers terrific views of Jack Mountain and the Colonial Peak massif. To the north, check out Ross Lake Resort, the line of floating cabins and bunkhouses that offer a magical getaway.

Going Farther

The Big Beaver Trail, a popular backpacking trail, continues for about 26 miles from the west side of Ross Dam. The first 6 miles follow the west shore of Ross Lake. Big Beaver Creek, about 6 miles from the dam, makes a good day-hike turnaround point.

Also nearby are Diablo Lake Trail, Hike 16, and Happy Creek Forest Walk (Hike 20).

Camping is available at Colonial Creek Campground on Highway 20. ∎

20. Happy Creek Forest Walk

RATING	DISTANCE	HIKING TIME
★★☆☆☆	**0.3-mile loop**	**20 minutes**
ELEVATION GAIN	**HIGH POINT**	**DIFFICULTY**
100 feet	**2,300 feet**	◆◇◇◇◇

BEST SEASON

Jan Feb Mar Apr May Jun **Jul Aug Sep Oct** Nov Dec

The Hike

This easy boardwalk loop takes you right into the heart of an ancient creekside forest environment. Interpretive signs detail the trail's firs, cedars, lichens, and, of course, the happy, bubbling creek. Benches let you take a load off, sit back, and just enjoy.

Getting There

Head east on Highway 20 (North Cascades Highway) to about mile post 134.4, about 14 miles east of Newhalem. The trailhead is on the right. Elevation: 2,200 feet.

Note: Most years, from late November to mid-April, miles 134 to 170 of Highway 20 are closed because of snow. Check www.wsdot .wa.gov for the latest conditions.

The Trail

Hop on the boardwalk and follow the loop clockwise as it snakes through massive, deep-furrowed Douglas firs and stately western red cedars, all hung for the holidays—and the whole year, actually—with

---

PERMITS/CONTACT
None required/North Cascades Visitor Center, (360) 854-7200

MAPS
USGS Ross Dam (trail not shown); Green Trails Diablo Dam 48

TRAIL NOTES
Leashed dogs okay; kid-friendly; wheelchair-accessible

Bridge spanning historic Ruby Creek

lichens and mosses. Check out the forest canopy for woodpeckers and the occasional flying squirrel. That canopy keeps visitors cool in summer and dry in spring and fall.

Interpretive signs fill in the blanks about recent fires (hence, the scattering of fire-scorched trees), lichens (old man's beard is so named because it looks like, what else? an old man's beard), and photosynthesis. Here's an interesting tidbit on our slimy slug friends: "Traveling on a film of mucus, the slug ventures from hideouts in the

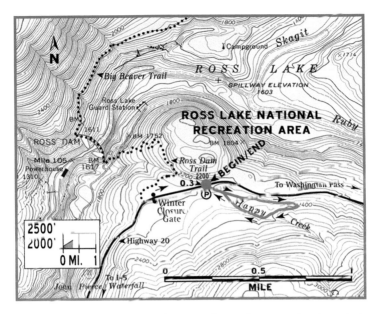

cool, moist hours to feed and mate." Funny, I've got a brother who's the same way.

Note. The boardwalk can be slippery when wet or frosty

Going Farther

Also nearby are Ross Dam Trail (Hike 19) and Big Beaver Trail.

Camping is available at Colonial Creek Campground on Highway 20. ∎

21. Ruby Creek Trail

RATING	DISTANCE	HIKING TIME
★★☆☆☆	2.2 miles round-trip	1 hour

ELEVATION GAIN	HIGH POINT	DIFFICULTY
200 feet	1,850 feet	◆◆◇◇◇

BEST SEASON
Jan Feb Mar Apr **May Jun Jul Aug Sep Oct** Nov Dec

The Hike

This less-traveled trail has all the ingredients for the perfect rainy-day hike: forested tree cover, a rushing creek, and a bit of history. Interpretive signs detail the creek's past as a late nineteenth-century gold-mining hot spot. An old sourdough found a good-sized ruby while panning at the water's edge, thus the creek's—and now the trail's—name.

Getting There

Head east on Highway 20 (North Cascades Highway) to milepost 138.4, about 18 miles east of Newhalem. The large trailhead parking lot is on the north (left) side of the road. Elevation: 1,850 feet.

Note: Most years, from late November to mid-April, miles 134 to 170 of Highway 20 are closed because of snow. Check www.wsdot.wa.gov for the latest conditions.

The Trail

Start by dropping about 200 feet, switchbacking for about 0.25 mile down through forest to the creek and a spiffy new wooden bridge. Interpretive signs detail the area's history, including that of George Holmes, who was born a slave in 1854 and who mined this creek from 1891 to 1925. Once across the bridge, at a T intersection turn right, following the sign for Ruby Creek Trail.

Follow as the shaded trail yo-yos a bit up and down along the rushing, gushing creek. At points you're looking down on the creek from 50 feet above; at others, you're leaving footprints on its sandy shore.

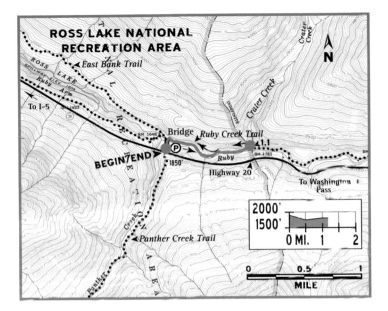

At several points, crystal-clear pools tempt you to pull up a boulder and contemplate that thing called life. Highway 20 is visible much of the way across the canyon, but for the most part you don't notice it because of the creek's ruckus-raisin'.

At **1.1** miles, just beyond the Ross Lake Recreational Area boundary marker, Crater Creek spills into Ruby Creek. This makes a good turnaround spot. Return the same way.

PERMITS/CONTACT
Northwest Forest Pass required/North Cascades Visitor Center,
(360) 854-7200

MAPS
USGS Crater Mountain; Green Trails Mount Logan 49

TRAIL NOTES
Leashed dogs okay; kid-friendly

Going Farther

The trail continues east for another 2.5 miles to the Canyon Creek trailhead, located on Highway 20 at milepost 141.3.

Another option is to go left after you cross the Ruby Creek bridge and pick up either the East Bank Trail, which eventually heads north for 30 miles along Ross Lake, or the trail that heads west along the south bank of Ruby Arm.

Also at the same trailhead, across the highway from the Ruby Creek Trail, is the Panther Creek Trail, which can be hiked up to Fourth of July Pass (Hike 18).

Camping is available at Colonial Creek Campground on Highway 20. ■

RAINY AND WASHINGTON PASSES

22. Easy Pass

RATING ★★★★★	DISTANCE 7.4 miles round-trip	HIKING TIME 5 hours
ELEVATION GAIN 2,900 feet	HIGH POINT 6,500 feet	DIFFICULTY ◆◆◆◆◇

BEST SEASON
Jan Feb Mar Apr May Jun **Jul Aug Sep Oct** Nov Dec

The Hike

Easy Pass isn't easy, but this hike isn't particularly hard either. And even if it were, the pass's spectacular views of Fisher Basin and glacier-heavy Mount Logan (and Mount Arriva and Fisher Peak and on and on) are more than worth it. Consider a fall visit when the larches are ablaze in gold.

Getting There

Head east on Highway 20 (North Cascades Highway) to milepost 151.5, 11 miles west of Washington Pass, about 32 miles east of Newhalem. At the well-signed spur road, turn right; the road-end trailhead is a couple hundred yards ahead. Elevation: 3,700 feet.

Note: Most years, from late November to mid-April, miles 134 to 170 of Highway 20 are closed because of snow. Check www.wsdot .wa.gov for the latest conditions.

PERMITS/CONTACT
Northwest Forest Pass required/Okanogan-Wenatchee National Forest, (509) 996-4000

MAPS
USGS Mount Arriva; Green Trails Mount Logan 49

TRAIL NOTES
Leashed dogs okay to national park boundary; great views

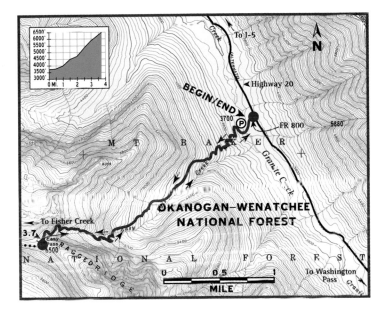

The Trail

After dropping into forest for a few hundred yards, come to Granite Creek. There's no bridge, so expect to get wet, at least to the knees, higher if it's a season of heavy spring runoff. Trekking poles are a capital idea. Once across, begin a steady switchback climb through silver fir and hemlock forest. Cross a couple of small creeks (which, oddly enough, have log bridges spanning them, unlike the aforementioned Mississippi-esque Granite Creek), pop in and out of forest a few times, and finally emerge into the open for good at about **2.3** miles.

Now begins the second act of today's program: the steep ascension of an oft-rocky gully, rimmed by the no-nonsense crags of Ragged Ridge. Much of the trail is on talus slope, and much of that doesn't like the look of your ankles or knees, so be careful with your footing—especially when coming down. The pass is the notch up ahead—between the rock on your right and the hard place on your left.

Views across Fisher Basin to Fisher Peak

At **3.7** miles, just after passing a post signaling your entry into North Cascades National Park, reach the heathery, peaceful pass. Views are way high on the Wow! scale. Across Fisher Basin, rock, snow, and ice are the mountains' dress code, and to the west Mount Logan shows off gleaming glaciers. From snowfields and glaciers on high, water tumbles down the basin, a place where the bear and the mountain goat roam.

Going Farther

Continue on the trail and drop about 1,300 feet in 2 miles to reach the Fisher Creek Trail. That trail continues for about 9 miles to Junction Camp and the Thunder Creek Trail (Hike 18). From there, several more options exist. ■

23. Lake Ann–Maple Pass Loop

RATING	DISTANCE	HIKING TIME
★ ★ ★ ★ ★	3.6- to 7.2-mile loop	5 hours

ELEVATION GAIN	HIGH POINT	DIFFICULTY
675 feet to 2,150 feet	6,850 feet	♦ ♦ ◊ ◊ ◊

BEST SEASON
Jan Feb Mar Apr May Jun **Jul Aug Sep Oct** Nov Dec

The Hike

If your tasks list includes: find yourself in the midst of countless Cascade peaks, tiptoe through wildflowers exploding with color, peer down into sparkling lakes and tumbling waterfalls stunning beyond all reason, then click on the Lake Ann–Maple Pass Loop. Another plus: "loop" means no doubling back. Definitely one of this book's top five trails.

Getting There

Head east on Highway 20 (North Cascades Highway) to milepost 157.6, about 5 miles west of Washington Pass, 37 miles east of Newhalem. Turn right at the Rainy Pass Picnic Area sign; the Lake Ann–Maple Pass trailhead is a few hundred yards ahead. Elevation: 4,800 feet.

Note: Most years, from late November to mid-April, miles 134 to 170 of Highway 20 are closed because of snow. Check www.wsdot.wa.gov for the latest conditions.

PERMITS/CONTACT
Northwest Forest Pass required/Okanogan-Wenatchee National Forest, (509) 996-4000

MAPS
USGS Washington Pass, Mount Arriva; Green Trails Mount Logan 49, Washington Pass 50

TRAIL NOTES
Leashed dogs okay; great views

Lake Ann below Maple Pass

The Trail

At the trailhead area, find the large sign for Lake Ann and start by following the smaller sign next to it that points the way to Maple Pass. Begin by climbing steadily and at times steeply through heavy timber. I once saw a lone male elk here with a gigantic rack, so big and unwieldy looking I wondered how he maneuvered it through the trees. It seemed as incongruous as seeing a sailboat in the woods. At **1.3** miles, arrive at a signed intersection with the Lake Ann Trail.

For Lake Ann: Take a left for a 0.5-mile (one-way) trail leading to this magical pond rimmed by huge rock walls. Once there, at **1.8** miles, look directly ahead and up, way up, 1,500 feet up—that's Maple Pass, where you'll be in a couple of hours. Imagine the view from up there. Better yet, head there. Return to the main trail at **2.3** miles.

For Maple Pass: Back on the main trail, the climb continues but at a mostly gentle rate. As you approach tree line, the forest thins and views down to Lake Ann and the surrounding cirque are stunning. And only get better. At **3.3** miles, after a short, steep stretch of elevation-gobbling switchbacks, reach Heather Pass, where there are campsites as well as great views of Black Peak to the northwest.

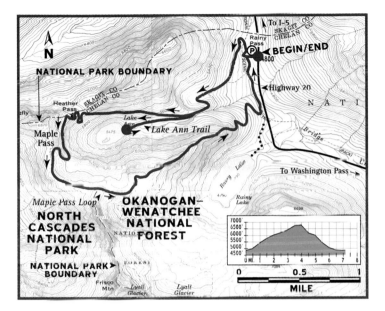

Continue onward and upward via some steep climbing, intoxicated by the mountain views and wildflower bouquets. Lake Ann is far, far below now, with Cutthroat Peak and a handful of other dry, reddish eastside Cascade peaks standing sentinel to the northeast. Reach Maple Pass at **4.1** miles (including the mile out and back to Lake Ann) and wow and whistle at views that have now—because you can see to the south—doubled in intensity and gigantic hugeness. Nearby Corteo Peak, kinda-far Dome Peak, and distant Glacier Peak jostle for attention in this sea of icy, glacier-clad summits that seem to stretch to infinity. Views and mountain wonder—as well as the biggest marmots I've ever seen—are all around you.

Continue following the obvious trail as it roller-coasters the ridge heading east until you come to the rim of a hanging basin where you pretty much have no choice but to head down. Frisco Mountain is above and to your right. Switchback down the somewhat exposed ridge and check out the huge horsetail waterfall plunging into Rainy

Lake—this trail has a little of everything! After reentering the forest, reach the paved Rainy Lake Trail at about **6.8** miles. Turn left to follow it back to the trailhead.

Going Farther

The Rainy Lake Trail (Hike 24), shares this trailhead. Camping is available at Lone Fir Campground, about 11 miles east on Highway 20. ■

24. Rainy Lake

RATING ★★★☆☆	DISTANCE 1.8 miles round-trip	HIKING TIME 1 hour
ELEVATION GAIN 50 feet	HIGH POINT 4,800 feet	DIFFICULTY ◆◇◇◇◇
BEST SEASON		
Jan Feb Mar Apr May Jun **Jul Aug Sep Oct** Nov Dec		

The Hike

This paved, flat, wheelchair-accessible trail dispels the notion that one must huff, puff, and bust a lung to earn top-notch views. With almost no effort, you're treated to peaceful, contemplative Rainy Lake, fed by a plunging, awe-inspiring horsetail of water—all enclosed by a rock- and glacier-rimmed cirque. The Rainy Lake Trail is also great for breaking up a long Highway 20 drive.

Getting There

Head east on Highway 20 (North Cascades Highway) to milepost 157.6, about 5 miles west of Washington Pass, 37 miles east of Newhalem. Turn right at the Rainy Pass Picnic Area sign; the trailhead is a few hundred yards ahead. Elevation: 4,800 feet.

Note: Most years, from late November to mid-April, miles 134 to 170 of Highway 20 are closed because of snow. Check www.wsdot .wa.gov for the latest conditions.

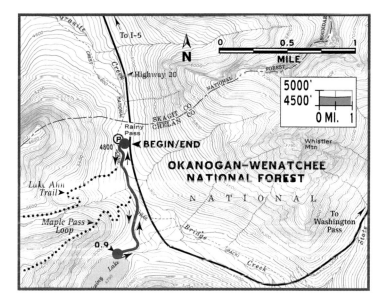

The Trail

At the big trailhead sign, bear left and follow the paved trail. Follow the path through forest, learning from one of many interpretive signs that you're hiking among Engelmann spruce and Pacific silver firs. Lichens and the like are discussed on another sign. Along the way, a number of benches offer respite. At **0.4** mile, at the intersection with the Lake Ann–Maple Pass Loop, continue straight.

PERMITS/CONTACT
Northwest Forest Pass required/Okanogan-Wenatchee National Forest, (509) 996-4000

MAPS
USGS Washington Pass (trail not shown); Green Trails Washington Pass 50

TRAIL NOTES
Leashed dogs okay; kid-friendly; good views; wheelchair-accessible

Just before reaching a paved viewing platform at **0.9** mile, you'll hear the snow- and glacier-fed waterfall splashing down the far side of Rainy Lake's basin. It sounds like rain. Though the falls are more than 0.5 mile away across the lake, you'll swear they're getting you wet. If you're a waterfall lover, this is one you won't want to miss. Return the same way.

Going Farther
The Rainy Pass Picnic Area is also the trailhead for the Lake Ann–Maple Pass Loop (Hike 23). Camping is available at Lone Fir Campground about 11 miles east on Highway 20. ∎

25. Blue Lake Trail

RATING	DISTANCE	HIKING TIME
★★★★☆	4.4 miles round-trip	2 hours
ELEVATION GAIN	HIGH POINT	DIFFICULTY
1,050 feet	6,250 feet	♦♦◇◇◇
BEST SEASON		
Jan Feb Mar Apr May Jun **Jul Aug Sep Oct** Nov Dec		

The Hike
Easy-access mountain magic is one way to describe this short jaunt to an alpine lake just backstage of the amazing Liberty Bell massif. Mountain views are truly stunning, as is the kaleidoscope of fall colors come September.

Getting There
Head east on Highway 20 (North Cascades Highway) to milepost 161.5, 0.8 mile west of Washington Pass. The trailhead is on the south side of the road. Elevation: 5,200 feet.

Note: Most years, from late November to mid-April, miles 134 to 170 of Highway 20 are closed because of snow. Check www.wsdot .wa.gov for the latest conditions.

Blue Lake on a bluebird day

The Trail

From behind the trailhead privy, head up into a spruce-heavy forest on the obvious trail. Hear them cars zooming by on Highway 20. That'll go away. Crossing damp spots via boardwalk, look up through breaks in the trees to the towering rock spires of Liberty Bell and the Early Winters massif. At **0.9** mile, reach a brief clearing where views whet one's appetite for what's to come. You've got your heathers, your wildflowers, your Cutthroat Peak and Whistler Mountain—it's getting to be quite a scene, really.

PERMITS/CONTACT
Northwest Forest Pass required/Okanogan-Wenatchee National Forest, (509) 996-4000

MAPS
USGS Washington Pass (trail not shown); Green Trails Washington Pass 50

TRAIL NOTES
Leashed dogs okay; kid-friendly; great views

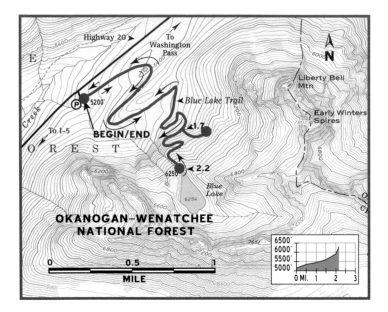

Return to forest complete with some very big boulders—castaways from Liberty Bell. At **1.7** miles, just after leaving the forest, ignore the trail leading to the left and up—that's the climbers' route for the Liberty Bell massif. The trail levels off for a short stretch before reaching a rushing stream requiring a potential wet-foot crossing. Picnic-perfect Blue Lake, rimmed on two sides by sky-high rock walls, is just ahead. After lunch, just try not to lie down beside the lazy turquoise tarn and take a nap. I dare you.

Return the same way. ∎

26. Washington Pass Overlook

RATING	DISTANCE	HIKING TIME
★★★★☆	0.25-mile loop	30 minutes

ELEVATION GAIN	HIGH POINT	DIFFICULTY
20 feet	5,620 feet	◆◇◇◇◇

BEST SEASON
Jan Feb Mar **Apr May Jun Jul Aug Sep Oct Nov** Dec

The Hike

Everyone has the potential to be an Ansel Adams on this short paved loop that offers you the front-row Liberty Bell views you've seen on a million postcards of the North Cascades. Interpretive signage tells the history of the North Cascades Highway, which opened in 1972. Interesting oddity: This is the only trail in the book with ashtrays along the way.

Getting There

Head east on Highway 20 (North Cascades Highway) to milepost 162.3, about 42 miles east of Newhalem. Turn north (left) at the sign for Washington Pass Overlook and follow the paved road for about 0.5 mile to a parking lot and picnic area. Elevation: 5,610 feet.

Note: Most years, from late November to mid-April, miles 134 to 170 of Highway 20 are closed because of snow. Check www.wsdot .wa.gov for the latest conditions.

PERMITS/CONTACT
None required/Okanogan-Wenatchee National Forest, (509) 996-4000

MAPS
USGS Washington Pass; Green Trails Washington Pass 50

TRAIL NOTES
Leashed dogs okay; kid-friendly; great views; wheelchair-accessible

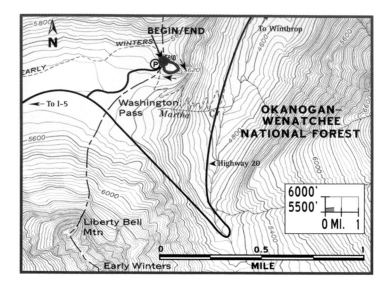

The Trail

Even before you've settled on which pocket to put your car keys in, the views from this trail will have loosened the hinges on your lower jaw. Less than two minutes from the car, emerge from trees onto a large rock outcropping that offers the Liberty Bell–Early Winters Spires panorama to the south. Stunning times ten. Views also of the Wine Spires, Kangaroo Ridge, Vasiliki Ridge, and Silver Star Mountain to the east. Look, but don't reach out to try to touch. Highway 20 is almost 700 feet straight down.

The view is complemented by a few lines of poet William Stafford's "A Valley Like This," set in stone:

> Please think about this as you go on. Breathe on the world.
> Hold out your hands to it. When mornings and evenings
> Roll along, watch how they open and close, how they
> Invite you to the long party that your life is.

Sound advice. ∎

27. Cutthroat Pass Trail

RATING	DISTANCE	HIKING TIME
★★★★★	11 to 11.5 miles round-trip	7 hours

ELEVATION GAIN	HIGH POINT	DIFFICULTY
2,500 feet	6,800 feet	♦♦♦♦♦

BEST SEASON
Jan Feb Mar Apr May Jun **Jul Aug Sep Oct** Nov Dec

The Hike

This is the story about a peaceful, cirque-surrounded mountain lake, a trail that gets you to almost 7,000 feet but doesn't run you ragged in the process, and views of both east- and west-side peaks that stretch to infinity. This trail intersects with one of the most scenic stretches of the Pacific Crest Trail.

Getting There

Head east on Highway 20 (North Cascades Highway) to milepost 167, about 4 miles east of Washington Pass, about 25 miles west of Winthrop. Turn left (west) onto Forest Road 400 and follow it for 1 mile to the road-end trailhead. Elevation: 4,500 feet.

Note: Most years, from late November to mid-April, miles 134 to 170 of Highway 20 are closed because of snow. Check www.wsdot .wa.gov for the latest conditions.

The Trail

Start by crossing Cutthroat Creek via a log bridge. Once across, luxuriate in the wide, well-maintained trail as it passes through eastside (read: dry-side) forest below an impressive but nameless rock ridge. Cutthroat Peak is visible from time to time through the trees

At about **1.7** miles, go left at a fork and in about 0.25 mile reach Cutthroat Lake, crossing a couple of creeks and passing a few campsites along the way. Ogle the towering rock wall surrounding the lake on almost all sides, with turretlike Cutthroat Peak watching over all. After exploring and reflecting, return to the main trail and resume your

Ridge overlooking Cutthroat Lake

journey to the pass. Almost as soon as you're back on the main trail at **2.2** miles, go right at an unsigned intersection that's just ahead.

The trail climbs steadily—switchbacks galore—but, for the most part, not steeply. As the forest thins the higher you go, the views become more expansive, especially to the south—Cutthroat Lake below, its peak above, and Silver Star and the steeples of the Liberty Bell massif beyond. To the east, jagged peaks seem to be everywhere in this arid, high country that's almost a photographic negative of the west (wet) side. In fall, the larches, which dominate here, put on a grand show as they turn gold.

Nearing the pass, cross some boulder fields and pass through massive rock slabs that are a haven for ground squirrels—they're everywhere. At **5.5** miles (6 miles if you made the side trip to the lake), reach the pass and the intersection with the Pacific Crest Trail.

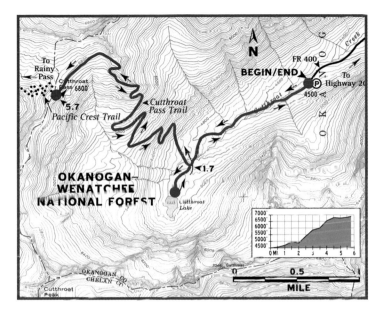

For even more scrumptious views, wander south on the PCT for a short way, where Cascade views seem to unfold themselves before your very eyes. Return the same way.

Going Farther
Because this trail leads to the Pacific Crest Trail, the possibilities for extending the hike either north or south are just about endless.

PERMITS/CONTACT
None required/Okanogan-Wenatchee National Forest, (509) 996-4000

MAPS
USGS Washington Pass; Green Trails Washington Pass 50

TRAIL NOTES
Leashed dogs okay; kid-friendly; great views; wheelchair-accessible

---

An alternate route to Cutthroat Pass is to hike the PCT north from the Rainy Pass trailhead, located at milepost 157.6, about 5 miles west of Washington Pass. To make this a one-way hike, leave from the Rainy Pass trailhead—see Lake Ann–Maple Pass Loop (Hike 23) and Rainy Lake (Hike 24)—hike north (and up) to Cutthroat Pass, then east (and down) to the Cutthroat trailhead. Total distance about 10.5 miles.

Camping is available at Lone Fir Campground on Highway 20. ■

HARTS PASS
AND THE METHOW

---

28. Driveway Butte

RATING	DISTANCE	HIKING TIME
★★★☆☆	8 miles round-trip	4 hours

ELEVATION GAIN	HIGH POINT	DIFFICULTY
3,100 feet	5,982 feet	♦♦♦♦◇

BEST SEASON
Jan Feb **Mar Apr May** Jun Jul Aug Sep Oct Nov Dec

The Hike

When other high-elevation trails are still buried under many feet of snow, 6,000-foot-high Driveway Butte offers an early-season mountain hiking experience. South facing and on the east side of Rainy Pass, this trail is often snow-free all the way to the top in May. Other pluses—ponderosa pines and sunflower fields forever.

Getting There

Head east on Highway 20 (North Cascades Highway) to just past milepost 175, about 13 miles east of Washington Pass, 18 miles west of Winthrop. Turn left on Forest Road 300, following the sign for a campground. (Though the sign on Highway 20 doesn't say so, it's Klipchuck Campground.) Follow the road for about a mile to the well-signed Driveway Butte trailhead parking lot on the right. Elevation: 3,000 feet.

PERMITS/CONTACT
Northwest Forest Pass required/Okanogan-Wenatchee National Forest, (509) 996-4000

MAPS
USGS Robinson Mountain, Silver Star Mountain; Green Trails Washington Pass 50

TRAIL NOTES
Leashed dogs okay; great views

Silver Star Mountain from Driveway Butte

The Trail

From the parking lot, follow the sign for Driveway Butte Trail. After a short stretch of new trail, take a right on the actual trail (signed), which follows an old skid road for the first 0.5 mile. This section is steep and one can't help but be curious about the days of yore when livestock were driven up this way to graze upon the mountain meadows in summer (hence the name "Driveway Butte"). Look for hoofprints in the dirt; apparently deer—which you're likely to see plenty of on this hike—like this trail as much as humans do.

After about **0.5** mile the trail lets up on its relentlessly steep attitude and segues into more gentle switchbacks. Note the glaciated massif that is Silver Star Mountain to the south and up. Note the unglaciated ribbon that is Highway 20 to the south and down. Note also that burning sensation you're likely to feel on your head and neck. It's called the sun. Much of this trail is unshaded and, because of its southern exposure and being on the east side of the Cascade Crest, it tends toward the bright and hot. (Lots of water and

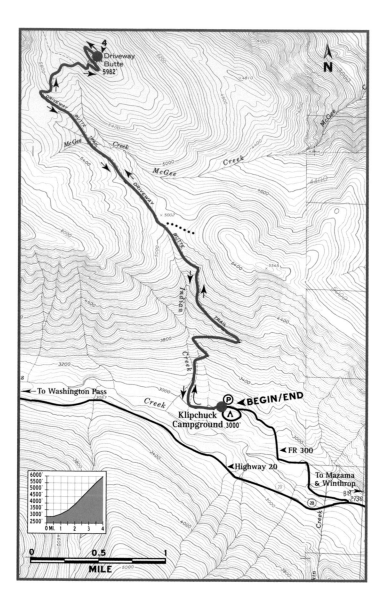

Sunflower Fields Forever

sunscreen are musts.) Note also sunflowers by the thousands (actually arrowleaf balsamroot). You'll find yourself amending the Beatles hit to "Sunflower Fields Forever" whether you're aware of it or not.

Pop back and forth between forest—note ponderosa pines and their rust-colored trunks—and sunflower meadows while gaining elevation at a healthy clip. At about **2.3** miles, after climbing more than 2,000 feet from the parking lot, reach the edge of a cool, forested saddle that is unlike anything you've come to so far. A small campsite (without water) is to the left and to the right, an unmarked trail leads about 0.75 mile to an unnamed butte about 450 feet lower than Driveway Butte. If you're not in the mood for the nearly 2 more miles to Driveway, head to the right for the anonymous peak Otherwise, continue straight ahead into cool, semi-damp woods that feature several muddy creek crossings and some potentially overgrown stretches. The grade here is much less steep than it has been to this point.

At **3.7** miles, exit the forest and find yourself at the base of the butte. ("Base of the butte"—that's fun to say.) Begin what is a strenuous, straight-up-the-mountain final push to the top, following cairns if the trail becomes sketchy. After climbing about 500 feet in a third of a mile, reach the top and the 360-degree views awaiting you. Silver Star, North Gardner Mountain, and the Early Winters area demand your attention, while the Pasayten Wilderness and Methow River valley patiently wait for you to turn around and offer them their props. Take note of the old concrete posts and other bits on the "summit" that allude to the old fire lookout that occupied this space until the 1950s.

Once you've OD'd on the views, return the same way.

Going Farther

Camping is available just past the trailhead parking lot at Klipchuck Campground. ■

29. Grasshopper Pass

RATING	DISTANCE	HIKING TIME
★★★★★	11 miles round-trip	6 hours
ELEVATION GAIN	**HIGH POINT**	**DIFFICULTY**
2,000 feet	7,125 feet	◆ ◆ ◇ ◇ ◇

BEST SEASON											
Jan	Feb	Mar	Apr	May	Jun	Jul	**Aug**	**Sep**	**Oct**	Nov	Dec

The Hike

Because your car has done most of the climbing in getting you to the trailhead, this above-tree-line alpine traverse affords spectacular mountain views almost the entire way. From long-distance views of Silver Star Mountain and the heart of the Pasayten Wilderness to reach-out-and-touch close-ups of Azurite Peak and Mount Ballard, Grasshopper Pass won't disappoint. Easy grade, too.

Getting There

Head east on Highway 20 (North Cascades Highway) to mile-post 179.5, about 59 miles east of Newhalem or 17 miles east of Washington Pass, and 13 miles west of Winthrop. Turn left (north) at the sign for Mazama, and in about 0.5 mile turn left again, following the sign for Harts Pass, which is 19 miles of mostly gravel—sometimes heart-stoppingly winding—road up the valley. One narrow, exposed stretch of road is the scariest road I've been on—that is, except for the last stretch of road to Slate Peak (Hike 30). At 9 miles bear right, following a sign for Harts Pass; 9.8 miles after that, at the sign for Meadows Campground, turn left onto Forest Road 500. The trailhead is 1.8 miles ahead. Elevation: 6,400 feet.

The Trail

After slogging through heavy timber for all of . . . 20 yards, reach the T intersection with the Pacific Crest Trail. Head left and start a wide-open traverse on which you'll swear you can see forever, and not just on clear days. Those from the west side of the Cascades will be intrigued by these gray, dusty, somewhat scrubby hills, folds, and ridges where trees are sparse but the flowers are not. It's a different brand of beauty from the moss-hung, evergreen forests to the west.

The trail traverses bowl after bowl—you can see it spread out for miles ahead of you—below a long, rocky skyline ridge. Gradual ups are followed by gradual downs that are followed by gradual ups. Et cetera. For about the first 2 miles you hike below the watchful eye

---

PERMITS/CONTACT
Northwest Forest Pass required/Okanogan-Wenatchee National Forest,
(509) 996-4000

MAPS
USGS Slate Peak; Green Trails Washington Pass 50

TRAIL NOTES
Leashed dogs okay; great views

A side trip from Grasshopper

of Tatie Peak, a high point along the skyline ridge on your right. To your left, Handcock Ridge dominates.

At about **3.5** miles, the trail begins a somewhat sharp descent, partially down slippery talus slope, ending about 0.5 mile later at a camp area. A creek here offers the opportunity for a water stop. Back on the trail, make up much of the elevation you just lost and at **5.0** miles reach Grasshopper Pass as the trail bends to the south. To the west, the glaciated Azurite Peak–Mount Ballard massif rises large (more than 8,000 feet) and close (less than 2 miles) and, since you haven't seen it earlier, seems to have emerged out of thin air.

The trail continues south (to Mexico, since it's the PCT) and starts to drop dramatically in about 0.25 mile. Just before the descent, find a faint trail to the left that continues up the ridgeline. After a semi-technical, but not dangerous, 0.25 mile, reach the top of a knob that affords spectacular 360-degree views as well as feeds your inner peak bagger. Count the wave upon wave of rocky peaks, jostling for props. Silver Star and the upper peaks of Early Winters Spires are among the too-many-to-count to the south. North-wise it's all ridgelines and valleys, humps and bumps that go on forever. Check out the Slate

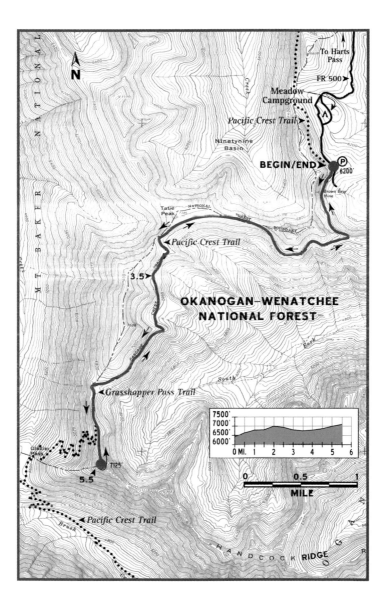

Peak Lookout and the road leading to it. It's the highest (and perhaps scariest) road in the state. Return the same way.

Going Farther
Because this hike follows the Pacific Crest Trail, the possibilities for extending your mountain fun are potentially limitless. The PCT offers numerous campsites too.

Camping is available at the Meadows Campground on FR 500 and at the Harts Pass Campground at Harts Pass. ■

30. Slate Peak

RATING	DISTANCE	HIKING TIME
★★★☆☆	0.5 mile round-trip	30 minutes
ELEVATION GAIN	**HIGH POINT**	**DIFFICULTY**
200 feet	7,440 feet	◆◇◇◇◇

BEST SEASON											
Jan	Feb	Mar	Apr	May	Jun	Jul	**Aug**	**Sep**	**Oct**	Nov	Dec

The Hike
Okay, so it's not really much of a hike. It's a 0.25-mile jaunt up a dirt road, but it's not just any dirt road—it's the highest public road in Washington State. And man, oh man, what mountain and valley views! There's nowhere that the sky seems bigger than from Slate Peak.

Getting There
Head east on Highway 20 (North Cascades Highway) to milepost 179.5, about 59 miles east of Newhalem and 13 miles west of Winthrop. Turn left (north) at the sign for Mazama, and in about 0.5 mile turn left again, following the sign for Harts Pass, which is 19 miles of mostly gravel—sometimes heart-stoppingly winding—road up the valley. At 9 miles bear right, following a sign for Harts Pass; 10 miles after that, arrive at Harts Pass and go right on Forest Road 600 for about 3 miles. The last 0.5 mile of this road is extremely exposed

Road to Slate Peak

and rocky. How rocky? In all the years I've spent writing guidebooks and driving rocky mountain roads, it's the only one on which I got a flat tire. How exposed is it? White knuckle, 200-heartbeats-per-minute exposed. Elevation: 7,240 feet.

The Trail

From the parking lot, pass around the gate, see the Slate Peak Lookout up ahead, and walk toward it. You'll be there in no time. Mountains and valleys are everywhere you turn your head—both emerald green and snow-covered (west and wet) and tawny and crag-topped (east) Cascades, as well as stretches of big-country Pasayten

PERMITS/CONTACT
None required/Okanogan-Wenatchee National Forest, (509) 996-4000

MAPS
USGS Slate Peak; Green Trails Washington Pass 50

TRAIL NOTES
Leashed dogs okay; kid-friendly; great views

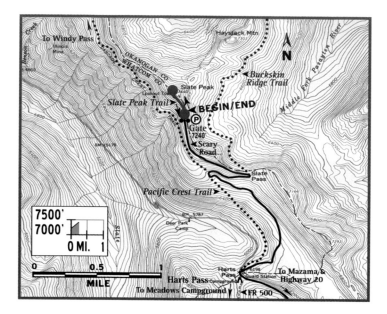

Wilderness as far as the eye can see. If you're taking mountain attendance, check off Mount Baker, Jack Mountain, Silver Star Mountain, Azurite Peak, and a few hundred others.

Reach the lookout, now used only in times of fire emergency, and reflect on the site's history. The first lookout here was built in the 1920s, but destroyed in the 1950s when the Air Force decided they wanted to use the site for an early detection radar system. They removed the top 40 feet of the peak (thus, the odd flatness of the summit) only to realize they wouldn't need the site after all; the warning system had become obsolete. Eventually the Forest Service moved back in and raised the lookout 41 feet. Return the same way.

Going Farther

A number of trails, including the Windy Pass section of the Pacific Crest Trail, pass through the Harts Pass area. The trailhead for 16-mile (one-way) Buckskin Ridge Trail is located about 2 miles north of Harts Pass on FR 600.

Camping is available at the Harts Pass Campground at Harts Pass. ■

31. Goat Peak Lookout

RATING	DISTANCE	HIKING TIME
★★★★	5 miles round trip	3 hours
ELEVATION GAIN	HIGH POINT	DIFFICULTY
1,900 feet	7,000 feet	♦♦♦♦

BEST SEASON
Jan Feb Mar Apr May Jun Jul Aug Sep Oct Nov Dec

The Hike

At Goat Peak, you're greeted by not only the finest views of the Methow Valley but also Lightnin' Bill, the friendliest fire lookout in the West. Views are of the high and eastside dry variety, with Silver Star Mountain dominating to the south. Bill's a poet too and if you're lucky he'll read you "Mountain Top Hop," his ode to staffing a lookout during a lightning storm. This is very dry country—you cross nary a creek—so be sure to take plenty of water.

Getting There

Head east on Highway 20 (North Cascades Highway) to milepost 179.5, about 59 miles east of Newhalem or 17 miles east of Washington Pass, and 13 miles west of Winthrop. Turn left (north) at the sign for Mazama, and in about 0.5 mile turn right, onto Lost River Road. In 2 miles, turn left onto gravel Forest Road 52. Follow it for 2.7 miles, then turn left onto FR 5225 and follow the sign for Goat Peak Lookout Trail. In 5.8 miles turn right, following the sign for FR 200, and reach the trailhead in 3 miles. Elevation: 5,600 feet.

Note: Cattle graze these hills, undeterred by what are called "fences." Don't be surprised to find yourself sharing the road with three or more bovine.

The Trail

Start by climbing up a mostly gentle slope through forest that offers the occasional glimpse south to Silver Star and Gardner Mountains. On the hills to the north, note the thousands of charred trees from a

Goat Peak Lookout overlooking the Methow Valley

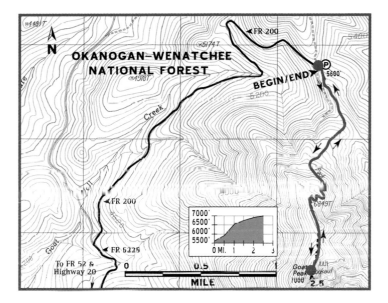

1994 forest fire. At about **0.7** mile cross an open meadow and make for that big, forested hump ahead of you—that's where the lookout is.

Once in the trees, the trail climbs very steeply and is at times rough. At **1.9** miles crest a mostly open ridge and put the tough climbing behind you. Mountain views are stunning and of the 360-degree variety. Follow a series of camel humps to the lookout straight ahead.

Goat Peak is one of the last staffed fire lookouts in the Methow Valley. The lookout is staffed by Ralph William Austin, a.k.a. Lightin' Bill. Bill, who's wanted to be a lookout ever since he was four or five years old, says that being inside a lookout tower during a lightning storm is like being inside a light bulb. We'll take his word for it. ∎

32. Sun Mountain Trails

RATING	DISTANCE	HIKING TIME
★★★★ ☆	**Varies**	**From 30 minutes to as long as you wish**
ELEVATION GAIN	HIGH POINT	DIFFICULTY
Varies	**2,900 feet**	◆ ◆ ◆ ◇ ◇

BEST SEASON
Jan Feb **Mar Apr May** Jun Jul Aug **Sep Oct Nov** Dec

The Hike

Set high atop the Methow Valley, Sun Mountain is not only the setting for the posh lodge that bears its name, but also a 40-mile network of trails that are maintained by the Methow Valley Sport Trails Association, Sun Mountain Lodge, and Okanogan–Wenatchee National Forest. Starting out high (2,900 feet), most offer spectacular Methow Valley and North Cascade views. In winter, many make terrific snowshoe and/or cross-country ski routes.

Getting There

Head east on Highway 20 (North Cascades Highway) to milepost 195, just past downtown Winthrop, about 33 miles past Washington Pass. Just after crossing a bridge spanning the Methow River, turn right onto Twin Lakes Road. Follow for 3 miles to Patterson Lake Road and turn right. Follow for about 6.4 miles to the Sun Mountain Lodge. Best to park at the far end near the tennis courts. Elevation: 2,900 feet.

The Trails

Sun Mountain is kind of the Methow's one-stop spot for all your trail needs—not only hiking, but mountain biking, horseback riding, trail-running, cross-country skiing, and snowshoeing as well. Trails start out relatively high—2,900 feet—and don't climb a whole lot, so they're accessible to a wide range of the hiking population. But the views are spectacular: wildflowers galore, mountains times ten,

Hikers heading out along the Kraule Trail

golden forests of western larch in fall, not to mention various creeks, rivers, and lakes to make the picture complete.

Because there are so many trails, space doesn't allow me to describe them all, so here are a few options to consider:

Kraule–Black Bear Loop: This 4.5-mile loop starts just past the tennis courts and traipses west atop a ridge through wildflower meadows with huge Methow Valley and North Cascade views. After about 1.5 miles, it enters pine forest and, after connecting with the Black Bear Trail (trails are signed), descends gently for a few hundred

PERMITS/CONTACT
None required/Sun Mountain Lodge, (509) 996-4735; Methow Valley Sport Trails Association, (509) 996-3287

MAPS
USGS Thompson Ridge; Green Trails Sun Mountain 03S

TRAIL NOTES
Kid-friendly; far-reaching views of the Methow Valley, North Cascades, and beyond; bikes and horses okay on some trails

feet while traversing the valley below. At **3.8** miles, go right on the Moose Trail and climb steeply for about 0.75 mile back to the Sun Mountain Lodge.

Interpretive Loop: This 0.75-mile ridgetop romp offers interpretive signs on the area's flora and fauna, as well as many of the same mountain-valley views to be had on more strenuous trails. This loop starts behind the tennis courts.

Patterson Lake–Rader Creek: This 5-mile loop starts just below the lodge at the Chickadee Trailhead. (To get there, turn left onto Thompson Ridge Road, about 1.2 miles before the lodge, or about 0.7 miles past Patterson Lake. The trailhead parking lot is just ahead.) Head south through forest for a few hundred yards before heading left onto the Cabin Trail and descending to the Patterson Lake Trail. At **0.8** miles, go right on the Patterson Lake Trail and follow as the cool, partially forested trail meanders slightly up and slightly down by the lake. Views across are to Patterson Mountain (Hike 33), the top to which you can climb if you're so inclined.

At **2.5** miles, turn right on the Rader Creek Trail and follow as the creekside route climbs gently up to a trail intersection at **4.0** miles.

Thompson Ridge, part of the Sun Mountain trail network, rises high above Patterson Lake

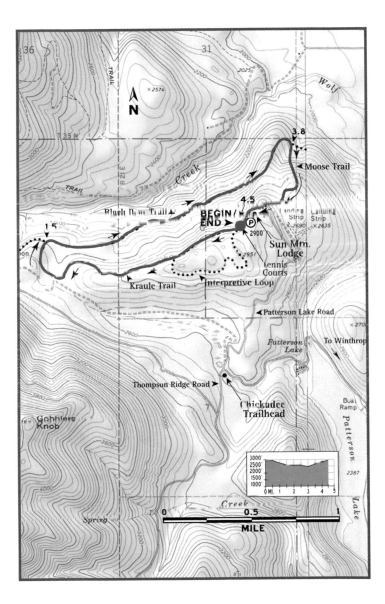

N

36
31

Wolf

35 N

T 35 N

TRAIL

R 21 E

×2574

3.8

Moose Trail

Creek

Black Dog Trail

4.5

BEGIN END

P

Landing Strip

Landing Strip

2900

×2690

×2635

1.5

2951

Sun Mtn. Lodge

Tennis Courts

Kraule Trail

Interpretive Loop

Patterson Lake Road

×270

Patterson Lake

To Winthrop

2600

Thompson Ridge Road

Chickadee Trailhead

Boat Ramp

Patterson Lake

Gohlberg Knob

2387

3000'
2500'
2000'
1500'
1000'

0 MI. 1 2 3 4 5

Creek

Spring

0   0.5   1

MILE

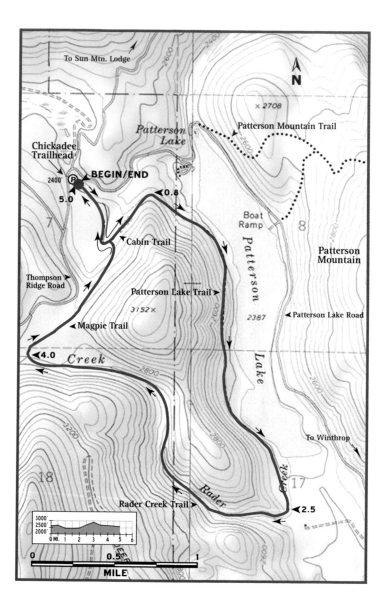

To Sun Mtn. Lodge

Patterson Lake

Patterson Mountain Trail

× 2708

Chickadee Trailhead

2400'

BEGIN/END

◄0.8

5.0

Cabin Trail

Boat Ramp

8

Patterson Mountain

Thompson Ridge Road

Patterson Lake Trail ►

Patterson

◄ Patterson Lake Road

3152×

2387

◄ Magpie Trail

Lake

◄4.0 Creek

To Winthrop

18

Rader

Creek

17

Rader Creek Trail ►

◄2.5

3000'
2500'
2000'

0 MI. 1 2 3 4 5 6

0   0.5   1
MILE

Pick up the Magpie Trail, and follow for about a mile back to the Chickadee Trailhead where you parked.

Going Farther

Patterson Mountain (Hike 33) is located about 2 miles south of Sun Mountain Lodge parking area. For suggestions on other Sun Mountain hiking options, go to the Sun Mountain Lodge Activity Room, located on the first floor. ■

33. Patterson Mountain

RATING	DISTANCE	HIKING TIME
★★★ ☆☆	4.6-mile loop	2.5 hours
ELEVATION GAIN	HIGH POINT	DIFFICULTY
1,200 feet	3,511 feet	◆◆◆

BEST SEASON
Jan Feb **Mar Apr May** Jun Jul Aug **Sep Oct Nov** Dec

The Hike

This short, not-too-strenuous loop trail outside Winthrop offers expansive Methow Valley views stretching from Mazama and the North Cascades at one end to Twisp and Eastern Washington at the other. There are sweet views of Patterson Lake directly below, too. This is a nice introduction to hiking for the kiddies.

Getting There

Head east on Highway 20 (North Cascades Highway) to milepost 195, just past downtown Winthrop, about 33 miles past Washington Pass. Just after crossing a bridge spanning the Methow River, turn right onto Twin Lakes Road. Follow for 3 miles to Patterson Lake Road and turn right. Follow for about 4.5 miles to Patterson Lake, which is on your left. Park at the signed boat launch area. Elevation: 2,400 feet.

PERMITS/CONTACT
None required/Methow Valley Sport Trails Association, (509) 996-3287;
Okanogan-Wenatchee National Forest, (509) 996-4003

MAPS
USGS Winthrop; Green Trails Sun Mountain 83S

TRAIL NOTES
Leashed dogs okay; kid-friendly; far-reaching views of the Methow Valley, North
Cascades, and beyond; no bikes

The Trail

Along with being known as a Nordic ski hotspot, the Methow Valley
is also popular with the mountain-biking set. Nothing against them,
of course, it's just nice to know you've got this mountain, on which
bikes are not allowed, to yourself—except for the cows in summer.
But that's another story.

From the boat launch area, cross Patterson Lake Road and head
up. Trees are at a minimum on this hill, which means 1) it's hot and

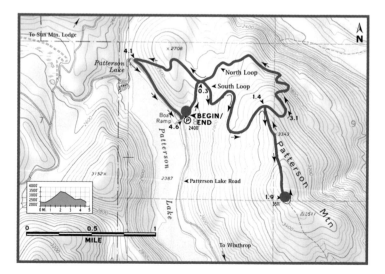

Patterson Lake at the foot of Patterson Mountain

dry in summer (take plenty of water) and 2) the views are great pretty much the whole way. At **0.3** miles, come to an intersection with a cattle gate and sign pointing to the north and south loops. Follow the South Loop, pass through the gate, and continue climbing through sunflower meadows or, if it's later in summer, meadows of post-bloom sunflower carcasses.

Terrific views below to Patterson Lake, Gardner Mountain beyond, and a host of other North Cascades increase with every step—which, by the way, are made a tad more difficult as the grade increases over the next mile. At **1.4** miles, reach a shoulder with the first views north to the Mazama-to-Winthrop stretch of the Methow Valley. A sign here points to the right and, as it says, leads to the summit, about another 300 feet up to the top of that hilly hummock on your right. If the little ones are game, go for it: it's about 0.5 mile each way and offers that hot-air-balloon-over-the–Methow Valley perspective. Otherwise continue straight (north) where the valley views are almost as good.

This is the North Loop of the trail and as you'll notice, it meanders in and out of forest, and in summer can feel 10 to 15 degrees

The North Cascades beckon just beyond the west reaches of the Methow Valley

cooler. (I was once here during the weekend of the Winthrop Rhythm and Blues Festival, and in the coolness of the forest I sat down to enjoy a couple tunes, which I could hear perfectly, being performed at the Blues Ranch down in the valley below. It was quite nice.) Views through the trees are stunning and of the North Cascade variety—Goat Peak where Lookout Bill holds sway, Robinson Mountain, and up toward Harts Pass.

Eventually, the trail starts descending steadily and at **2.1** miles (**3.1** if you hiked to the summit and back), you climb a stepladder that gets you through an opening in the cattle fence. (In summers, cattle are grazed here and this fence keeps them from getting into places they're not supposed to.) Continue down, traversing across the north and west side of the mountain with foreground views to the posh Sun Mountain Lodge, which is about a mile away as the cow flies. (If cows could fly, that is.)

Just ahead, reach the North Loop–South Loop intersection, gate included. For variety, head to the right and follow as the trail descends across the hill ending up at the north end of Patterson Lake at **3.1** (or **4.1**) miles. To get back to where you parked, walk the road for about 0.5 mile.

Going Farther

The trails at Sun Mountain Lodge (Hike 32) are accessed about 2 miles farther up Patterson Lake Road. ■

34. Slate Creek Trail

RATING	DISTANCE	HIKING TIME
★★★★☆	10 miles round-trip	6 hours
ELEVATION GAIN	**HIGH POINT**	**DIFFICULTY**
4,400 feet	6,705 feet	✦✦✦✦

BEST SEASON
Jan Feb Mar **Apr May** Jun Jul Aug **Sep Oct Nov** Dec

The Hike

Before the true heat of summer hits, this expressway to Abernathy Ridge and the Lake Chelen–Sawtooth Wilderness offers a great early season mountain fix—and a mega-quad workout too. This steep trail leaves the valley quickly but rewards with great views and a cool little pool, Slate Lake, by which to contemplate the wonder of it all. Or cast a line if you're so inclined.

Getting There

Head east on Highway 20 (North Cascades Highway) to milepost 201 and the town of Twisp, about 39 miles past Washington Pass. About 0.5 mile after entering the town proper, look for the Twisp River Recreation Area sign and turn right onto Twisp Road. Follow for 16.7 miles (the road becomes Forest Road 44 after about 12 miles) and turn right at the sign for Slate Creek Trail. The road-end trailhead is about 100 yards ahead. Elevation: 2,900 feet.

The Trail

From the trailhead sign that details all the things you can and cannot do or bring on this wilderness-entering trail (no geocaching, motorcycles, or chainsaws), head up into the dense pine and Doug fir forest. In a couple hundred yards, go straight at the intersection with the Twisp River Trail, a mostly flat forest walk (or mountain bike or horseback ride) that parallels the Twisp River for about 8 miles.

Back to our Slate Creek Trail—as you proceed, you'll soon notice something: you're forced to raise your knees and quads a bit higher than you would if you were say, walking down your front walkway to retrieve the newspaper. That's because the trail climbs steeply. Relentlessly. Without letup. And all that. Just take your time and enjoy the experience; the lake and the glorious ridgetop views aren't going anywhere. And from time to time, the trail passes through wildflower meadows, made especially impressive in the spring when the sunflowers (Arrowleaf balsamroot) are ablaze.

Speaking of views, because the forest is semi-open, impressive views west and south to the surrounding peaks and down into the Twisp River valley can be had much of the way. At about **1.5** miles, the trail rounds a bend, enters the Lake Chelan–Sawtooth Wilderness, and offers views north and east toward the Little Slate Creek drainage and Midnight and Three A.M. mountains.

The higher you go, the more the views open up until at about **3.0** miles you pop out of the forest at about 6,600 feet. The 360-degree views here are spectacular: out along Abernathy Ridge (which you've now attained) and across the Twisp River valley to Reynolds Peak, the prominent two-pronged mountain to the south. There are views to the far flat horizon of deep Eastern Washington, too.

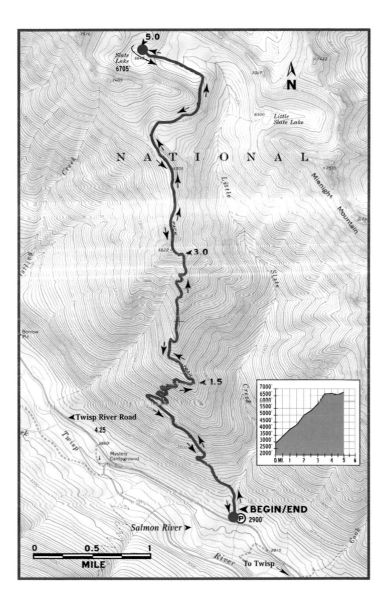

5.0

Slate Lake
6705'

N

Little Slate Lake

N A T I O N A L

Midnight Mountain

Little Slate Creek

Slate Creek

3.0

Borrow Pit

1.5

◄ **Twisp River Road**
4.25

Mystery Campground

◄ **BEGIN/END**
Ⓟ **2900'**

Salmon River ►

To Twisp

River

Crook Creek

0   0.5   1
MILE

7000'
6500'
6000'
5500'
5000'
4500'
4000'
3500'
3000'
2500'
2000'
0 MI. 1 2 3 4 5 6

Views south across the Twisp River include Reynolds Peak

If you're a vista bagger and/or in a time crunch, turn around here. Lake baggers continue on the ridge for 2 more spectacular ridge-walking miles—climbing and dropping some but not much—before reaching Slate Lake at **5.0** miles. Return the same way being careful, way careful, on the steep descent.

Going Farther

The 8-mile (one way) Twisp River Trail can be accessed at the same trailhead. Lookout Mountain (Hike 35) is accessed via Lookout Road, also off Twisp Road, about 16 miles east of the Slate Creek trailhead.

Camping is available at several campgrounds along Twisp Road (FR 44) including Mystery Campground, about 1 mile west of the trailhead, and War Creek Campground, about 3.5 miles east. ■

35. Lookout Mountain Trail (near Twisp)

RATING	DISTANCE	HIKING TIME
★ ★ ★ ☆ ☆	3.0 miles round-trip	1.5 hours

ELEVATION GAIN	HIGH POINT	DIFFICULTY
1,200 feet	5,600 feet	◆ ◆ ◆ ◇ ◇

BEST SEASON											
Jan	Feb	Mar	Apr	May	Jun	Jul	Aug	Sep	Oct	Nov	Dec

The Hike

Visits to fire lookout towers are always fun, even if they're closed and shuttered up like this one. That's because the views are as panoramic and wide open as they get, just as they are on this short, family-friendly hike. Plus, this trail borders some open rangeland so you might get to see some cows. Goody.

Getting There

Head east on Highway 20 (North Cascades Highway) to milepost 201 and the town of Twisp, about 39 miles past Washington Pass. About a half-mile after entering the town proper, look for the Twisp River Recreation Area sign and turn right onto Twisp Road. About a half-mile farther, turn left at the sign for Lookout Place. Follow as the road climbs, turns to gravel, and becomes more rugged, and after about 2 miles becomes Forest Road 200. Continue another 4 miles (6 miles in all) to the road-end parking lot. Note: There is a small area for maybe two cars about 50 feet up and to the left of the main parking lot. Turnaround space is limited so best to park in the main parking area. Elevation: 4,400 feet.

The Trail

Sure, this trail might be a tad steep for small kids—1,200 feet climbing in about a mile and a half, but it's short. And you just know the youngins will get a kick out of the fire lookout tower. That said, follow

From Lookout Mountain, views extend far into Eastern Washington

the road around the bend to the mini parking area and continue up through pine and fir forest on an old roadbed that soon enough narrows down to trail.

Enjoy the semi-open views of the Methow Valley, which only increase in Wow! quotient the higher you go. At your feet, depending on when you visit, flowers should be plentiful: lupine, paintbrush, and myriad others. Take note of the barbed wire fence to the right and, at about **0.5** mile, the cattle grate you walk over. This is a range area up here—the bovine like their mountain vistas as much as anyone—and the fence and grate are to keep the cattle from wandering where they're not supposed to.

At about **1.3** miles, the grade lessens as the trail contours to the south along Lookout Ridge. Views here are magnificent and will only get better when you reach that boxy structure on stilts— the lookout tower—about a quarter-mile up the ridge to the left.

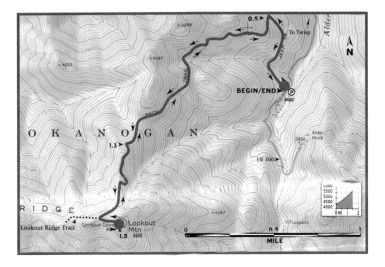

(Ignore the Lookout Ridge Trail that intersects here and leads off to the right.)

Staffed during fire emergencies only, the lookout site offers an expansive 360-degree vista of seemingly every nook and cranny in the Lake Chelan–Sawtooth Wilderness, Okanogan-Wenatchee National Forest, Methow Valley, and far beyond. Hoodoo Peak, fun to say, is the prominent one in the Sawtooth mountain range to the south. Look far west for the gateway peaks and crags of the North Cascades.

PERMITS/CONTACT
Northwest Forest Pass required/Okanogan-Wenatchee National Forest, (509) 996-4000

MAPS
USGS Twisp West; Green Trails Twisp 84

TRAIL NOTES
Leashed dogs okay; kid-friendly; far-reaching views of the Methow Valley, North Cascades, and beyond; bikes and horses okay; fire lookout tower

Hang out; there're a few benches providing a place to lunch. Soak in the views; there are lots of them. Return the same way.

Going Farther

The Lookout Ridge Trail continues west from the 1.3-mile mark for about 4 miles.

Camping is available at several campgrounds along Twisp Road, the closest being War Creek Campground located at about milepost 12.7.

Before the true heat of summer hits, this expressway to Abernathy Ridge and the Lake Chelen–Sawtooth Wilderness offers a great early season mountain fix—and a mega–quad workout too. This steep trail leaves the valley quickly but rewards with great views and a cool little pool, Slate Lake, by which to contemplate the wonder of it all. Or cast a line if you're so inclined. ■

CHUCKANUT AND BLANCHARD MOUNTAINS

36. Bat Caves

RATING	DISTANCE	HIKING TIME
★★★☆☆	7 miles round-trip	4 hours

ELEVATION GAIN	HIGH POINT	DIFFICULTY
2,000 feet	2,085 feet	◆◆◇◇◇

BEST SEASON
Jan Feb Mar Apr May Jun Jul Aug Sep Oct Nov Dec

The Hike

Simply put, Bat Caves Trail on Blanchard Mountain offers the best that Bellingham-area trails have to offer. Like routes on Chuckanut Mountain, Blanchard's northern cousin, Bat Caves (referred to in some books as Oyster Dome) offers emerald-isle views, but here they're from atop a 300-foot rock cliff.

Getting There

From Interstate 5, take exit 231 in Burlington. Drive north on Highway 11 (Chuckanut Drive) to about 100 yards north of milepost 10. The roadside pullout is on the west (left) side of the road. Elevation: 150 feet.

The Trail

At the trailhead, a Pacific Northwest Trail (PNT) rock informs that the Rocky Mountains are 883 miles of trail to the east, the Pacific Ocean

PERMITS/CONTACT
Discover Pass required/Department of Natural Resources, Northwest Region, (360) 856-3500

MAPS
USGS Bellingham South, Bow; Amazing Maps Chuckanut Mountains Blanchard Map

TRAIL NOTES
Leashed dogs okay; great views; bikes okay

Welcome to the Oyster Dome

223 trail miles west. Because the Bat Caves trail follows the PNT for a few miles, make sure you don't miss any turns or you might end up in Montana.

That said, start by switchbacking steeply up a forested hill that soon leaves the sounds of Chuckanut Drive behind. At **1.0** mile, reach a clearcut area that offers the first of the island and water views. Anacortes and a bunch of San Juan Islands are right there across Samish Bay. Views are quite grand and will only get better higher up.

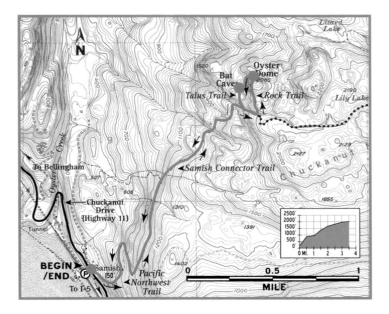

Check overhead for red-tailed hawks, bald eagles, and hang gliders riding the thermals.

At **1.6** miles reach an intersection with a somewhat confusing sign; continue straight. Now on the Samish Connector Trail, your route has become narrower, rockier, and more root-strewn. (It's nothing personal, just the way things are.) Cross a number of creeks and continue climbing, now fairly steeply. At another intersection continue straight and, as the trail becomes steeper, narrower, and, in general, more technical, be ready to use your hands in spots.

Spot the giant boulder with a nearby Ice Age interpretive sign at about **2.3** miles. The rock is fun to scramble up for decent water views, but the top of the dome is not far ahead so don't break out the wine and cheese just yet. After about 0.5 mile of more steep, rugged travel, go left on the signed Rock Trail. The top of the Dome is a little less than 0.5 mile ahead. Keep a leash on the pets and a hand on the kids and anything else that can't fly—it's a long way down.

Views are stupendous—the Olympics, the islands, the Sound, et cetera. Bust out the eats 'n' drinks.

Going Farther

The Oyster Dome rock wall is a popular local rock climbing destination, but requires technical equipment and skill.

Camping is allowed at nearby Lily and Lizard Lakes, and at Larrabee State Park, about 5 miles north. ■

37. Fragrance Lake

RATING	DISTANCE	HIKING TIME
★ ★ ★	5.2-mile lollipop loop	2.5 hours
ELEVATION GAIN	HIGH POINT	DIFFICULTY
1,050 feet	1,230 feet	♦ ♦
BEST SEASON		
Jan Feb Mar Apr May Jun Jul Aug Sep Oct Nov Dec		

The Hike

It's debatable whether Chuckanut Mountain is truly a part of the Cascades, but this fact can't be argued: It's one of only two inland Washington mountains that rise right straight up out of Puget Sound. (Blanchard Mountain, just to the south, is the other.) This forested trail tours the best that Chuckanut has to offer and culminates with a peaceful loop around a forest- and rock-rimmed mountain lake.

Getting There

From Interstate 5, take exit 231 in Burlington. Drive north on Highway 11 (Chuckanut Drive) to milepost 14.7. The obvious trailhead parking lot is on your right. If the lot is full, park across the street at Larrabee State Park. Elevation: 180 feet.

The view out toward the San Juan Islands

The Trail

Start by making a short, steep switchback climb that levels off at an intersection with the Interurban Trail, an old rail trail that stretches from Bellingham to Larrabee State Park. Pick up the Fragrance Lake Trail about 10 yards to the right, made obvious by the bike barricade. After a short, level prelude allowing you to acquaint yourself with your surroundings—dense shut-out-the-sky forest of thick-trunked hemlocks and cedars, sword ferns, and big, moss-wrapped boulders—the trail switchbacks onward and upward.

At **0.9** mile, come to a signed T intersection. Take a left and in a level hundred yards, reach a viewpoint that takes full advantage

PERMITS/CONTACT
Discover Pass required/Larrabee State Park, (360) 676-2093

MAPS
USGS Bellingham South; Chuckanut (Local Knowledge Trail Map)

TRAIL NOTES
Leashed dogs okay; kid-friendly; great views

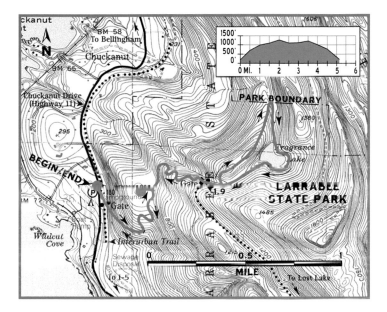

of Chuckanut Mountain's emergence from Samish Bay. See emerald isles—San Juan, Gulf, and Vancouver—snowcapped mountains, and lots of sun-sparkling water—northern Puget Sound and the Strait of Georgia. See also smooth-trunked madrona trees that'll convince you you're standing on one of the San Juans. Back on the main trail, continue to the right at the intersection, following the sign for Fragrance Lake; it's not much more than a mile away.

Though still a cinch to follow, the trail seems more rugged, the trees bigger, the moss mossier, the boulders bolder—some right on the trail almost. Watch for owls on this stretch; I often spot gray or great-horned owls here. At **1.9** miles reach an almost-always muddy notch with another bike barricade. Fragrance Lake is in a basin about 0.2 mile straight ahead. This peaceful, contemplative pond is circled by a 0.75-mile trail that offers plenty of access spots for fishing, swimming, or just doing that stare-at-the-water thing. Impressive sandstone cliffs too, on the north and northwest sides of the lake.

Before heading down into the lake basin, however, consider taking the more challenging trail that heads to the left and up just after the bike barricade. Climbing steeply at first, this at-times overgrown path leads to the top of those sandstone cliffs about 200 feet above the lake. The lake is visible at several points, but be careful—there's no guardrail and it's a long drop; I know of at least two dogs that discovered they couldn't fly here. At about **2.4** miles, the trail intersects with a more prominent—if unnamed—trail. Go right and reach the lakeshore in a couple hundred yards. Continue clockwise around the lake for about 0.5 mile and head left when the trail climbs out of the basin and up toward the second bike barricade—the stick of this lollipop loop. Return the same way from here.

Going Farther

To get to Lost Lake, another secluded Chuckanut Mountain pond, take a right at the second bike barricade and another just ahead in the obvious clearing, a former parking lot. In a couple hundred yards, go left on an old road, following the sign for Lost Lake. After about 1.2 miles of steady climbing, followed by the same distance of steady dropping, you'll reach the lake.

Camping is available across Chuckanut Drive at Larrabee State Park. ■

WEST MOUNT BAKER

38. Canyon Lake

RATING	DISTANCE	HIKING TIME
★ ★ ★ ☆ ☆	8.3-mile lollipop loop	5 hours
ELEVATION GAIN	**HIGH POINT**	**DIFFICULTY**
2,400 feet	4,560 feet	♦ ♦ ◇ ◇ ◇
BEST SEASON		
Jan Feb Mar Apr May Jun **Jul Aug Sep Oct** Nov Dec		

The Hike

Opened in 2001, this trail follows an old logging road to a 700-acre old-growth stand of Alaska yellow cedar, hemlock, and Pacific silver fir. Thank you, Paul Allen, for ponying up much of the dough so that this very special forest could be set aside. Great Mount Baker and Twin Sisters views too.

Getting There

Head east on Highway 542 (Mount Baker Highway) to milepost 16.8 and turn right onto Mosquito Lake Road. Follow it for 1.7 miles and turn left on gravel Canyon Lake Road, following the sign for Canyon Lake Creek Community Forest. Continue for 6.7 miles to the road-end parking lot. Elevation: 2,350 feet. (Note: As of press time, a 2009 storm washed out sections of Canyon Lake Road so now reaching the trailhead requires a 5.7-mile hike.)

The Trail

From the parking lot, you can visit peaceful, alpine Canyon Lake, then head for higher ground where spectacular mountain views and ancient trees await. The snags poking through Canyon Lake are the result of a nineteenth-century earthquake in which a forested hillside slid into the canyon, creating a natural dam.

When you're ready to make for the ridge and forest, find the old logging road and head up at a very gentle grade. Cross a number of new wooden bridges, many crossing rushing streams, and eventually leave the lake behind and below. Views emerge to the north (behind

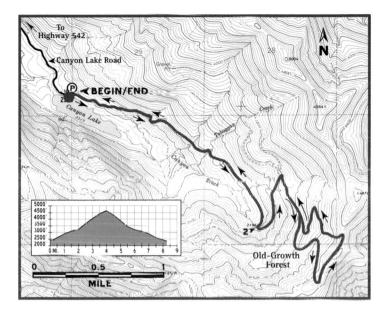

you) of the North Fork Nooksack River valley. Because much of the trail/road is at the edge of forest or in the open, don't expect to be shielded from the elements, be they rain or sun.

At about **2.0** miles, the trail steepens and begins switchbacking up out of the canyon. In summer 2001 large boulders blocking entrances to retired logging roads kept hikers on course. Cairns also marked the way. At about **3.0** miles, at an elevation of about 3,800 feet, leave

PERMITS/CONTACT
None required/Whatcom County Parks and Recreation, (360) 733-2900

MAPS
USGS Canyon Lake (trail not shown)

TRAIL NOTES
Leashed dogs okay; great views

Mount Baker flanked by the Black Buttes

the old road and follow the cairn-marked trail leading off to the right into the old-growth forest. Things get dark in a hurry. The needle-strewn dirt trail snakes through a forest of yellow cedars, hemlocks, and silver firs that many believe are up to 1,000 years old. Because of the relatively high elevation of such a forest, the trees, despite their age, are not the giants one might expect. Still, they are stately, grand, and tenacious—they've had dibs on the place for centuries.

Climb steadily through the forest and at 4.2 miles, reach a ridge-top former logging road that offers spectacular crevasse-counting views east to Mount Baker, south to the North Twin Sister, and west to the San Juan Islands and Olympic Mountains. Return the same way (for 8.4 miles round-trip) or, to make a loop, go left at the ridge. In about 0.3 mile, at another old logging road (which is actually the same one you started out on), go left and follow it all the way back to the parking lot. ∎

39. Heliotrope Ridge Trail

RATING	DISTANCE	HIKING TIME
★ ★ ★ ★	6.0 miles round-trip	4 hours
ELEVATION GAIN	**HIGH POINT**	**DIFFICULTY**
1,900 feet	5,600 feet	♦ ♦ ◇ ◇ ◇

BEST SEASON
Jan Feb Mar Apr May Jun **Jul Aug Sep Oct** Nov Dec

The Hike

Were this trail a Fox-TV special, it might be called "When hikers tickle the toes of glaciers!" or "When marmots whistle at mountain lovers!" or "When rushing creeks soak shoes and socks!"—all of which happen here. This popular trail rewards with an up-close-and-personal audience with Mount Baker's Coleman Glacier.

Getting There

Head east on Highway 542 (Mount Baker Highway) to milepost 34.3, about a mile east of the Glacier Public Service Center. Turn right onto Glacier Creek Road (Forest Road 39) and follow it for 8 miles, as the winding road alternates between pavement and gravel, to the road-end parking lot. Elevation: 3,700 feet.

The Trail

Upon entering the deep forest, drop down and cross rushing Grouse Creek via a handrail-less log bridge. If little ones are along, hold their hands and don't let go. Begin climbing steadily up a rocky, root-riddled, but well-maintained trail, crossing some wet spots via log bridges. Occasional breaks in the trees offer glimpses to Bastile Ridge and a few other glacier-made landforms.

At about **1.1** miles, after a brief, mostly level stretch, negotiate the first of several bridgeless creek crossings. In early summer especially, these creeks increase in volume and intensity as the day wears on, so trekking poles, as well as waterproof boots and/or gaiters, are a good idea. Return to climbing via switchbacks and within about

Mount Baker's icy-blue Coleman Glacier

0.5 mile, come to two more rushing, rock-hopper creek crossings, the second one especially wide (not to mention cold). You'll find yourself studying and strategizing before you make your move. After some more steep switchbacks, pass a couple of campsites as well as the old Kulshan Cabin site. At about **2.4** miles, pop out of the forest and treat yourself to some tasty Mount Baker views, bud.

Day-hike trail: Continue straight on the main trail for about 0.5 mile, letting massive Mount Baker draw you in. Take care when

---

PERMITS/CONTACT
Northwest Forest Pass required/Mount Baker–Snoqualmie National Forest, Glacier Public Service Center, (360) 599-2714

MAPS
USGS Groat Mountain; Green Trails Mount Baker 13

TRAIL NOTES
Leashed dogs okay; great views

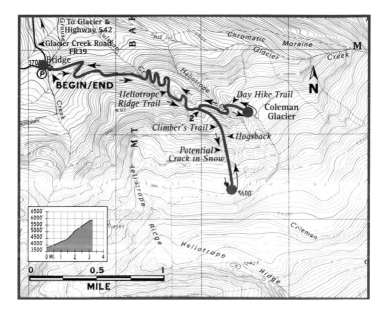

crossing snow and the various braids of Heliotrope Creek. The closer you get, the more your jaw involuntarily drops at the Coleman Glacier's otherworldly blue ice above, ahead, and even below you. The stacks of seracs—like giant snow mattresses just about to tumble—are stunning. The whistles you hear are marmots—some of the cheekiest anywhere—that call this moraine environment home. Return the way you came.

Climbers' trail: From the junction at about **2.4** miles, go to the right on a climbers' trail used by those planning to summit Mount Baker via the Coleman Glacier route. As long as day hikers stay off the glacier and don't proceed farther than the obvious hogsback about 0.5 mile farther, it's a fun day-trip destination. Warning: In spring and early summer, a meltwater creek and waterfall in a snowfield just west of the hogsback (at about 5,400 feet) create a crack in the snow that is hard to see from higher up. Unsuspecting snow revelers often glissade down the snowfield, thinking they have a clear runout, only to fall in the crack, which is about 25 feet deep. Tragically, in recent years, several people have fallen to their deaths. Do not, under any circumstances, glissade, ski, or snowboard here. Stay on the hogsback!

Going Farther
Horseshoe Bend Trail starts across from Douglas Fir Campground, where camping is available, about 1 mile east of Glacier Creek Road (FR 39). ∎

40. Boyd Creek Interpretive Trail

RATING	DISTANCE	HIKING TIME
★★☆☆☆	0.5 mile round-trip	20 minutes
ELEVATION GAIN	**HIGH POINT**	**DIFFICULTY**
20 feet	1,260 feet	◆◇◇◇◇
BEST SEASON		
Jan Feb Mar Apr May Jun Jul Aug Sep Oct Nov Dec		

The Hike
This creekside trail tells a fish tale, that of the anadromous types—saltwater swimmers/freshwater spawners—that call the Northwest's creeks and rivers home. Interpretive signs along the forested boardwalk detail the stream's ecology, including the life cycles of salmon and trout. A nice rainy-day outing.

Getting There
Head east on Highway 542 (Mount Baker Highway) to milepost 34.3, about 1 mile east of the Glacier Public Service Center. Turn right onto Glacier Creek Road (Forest Road 39) and, almost immediately, turn left onto FR 37. Follow it for 3.3 miles to the trailhead parking lot on the right. Elevation: 1,240 feet.

Reading a fish tale

The Trail

Views north from the trailhead are extraordinary. Below Church Mountain's craggy steeple, the powerful North Fork of the Nooksack River snakes its way around a bend. From the large interpretive trailhead sign, follow the wide, hard-packed dirt trail into the cool, damp forest. In about 75 yards, reach the first viewing area, which looks down into bubbling, babbling Boyd Creek. At various times

PERMITS/CONTACT
None required/Mount Baker–Snoqualmie
National Forest, Glacier Public Service Center, (360) 599-2714 (summer);
(360) 856-5700 (year-round)

MAPS
USGS Bearpaw Mountain (trail not shown);
Green Trails Mount Baker 13 (trail not shown)

TRAIL NOTES
Leashed dogs okay; kid-friendly; wheelchair-accessible

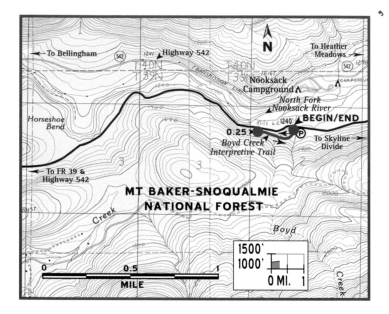

throughout the year, visitors can watch such species as chinook, pink, and coho salmon and steelhead and cutthroat trout in states of spawn.

From the first viewing area, the trail becomes an elevated boardwalk and heads to the right. Caution: It doesn't take much moisture—either in the form of rain or frost—for this boardwalk to become extremely slippery. Because most of the trail is shaded, expect it to be slick.

More interpretive signs can be found, as well as occasional glimpses high above to Church Mountain. Look for rock-hopping American dippers, sparrow-size birds that dive-bomb the creek for insects. At about **0.25** mile, the trail ends at a viewing area. Look south through cedars and alders for views of the creek spilling down the hillside.

Mount Baker from Skyline Divide

Going Farther

Horseshoe Bend Trail starts across from Douglas Fir Campground, where camping is available, about 1 mile east of Glacier Creek Road (FR 39). ∎

41. Skyline Divide Trail

RATING	DISTANCE	HIKING TIME
★★★★★	7-plus miles round-trip	4-plus hours

ELEVATION GAIN	HIGH POINT	DIFFICULTY
2,100 feet	6,250 feet	◆◆◇◇◇

BEST SEASON
Jan Feb Mar Apr May Jun **Jul Aug Sep Oct** Nov Dec

The Hike

"Just a little bit farther." That's the phrase you repeat over and over whilst ambling this ridge-top meadow where flowers and mountain views transport you to another world. Massive Mount Baker, so close it's as big as the sky itself, pulls you along. The-hills-are-alive-with-the-sound-of-music quotient is seriously high here.

Getting There

Head east on Highway 542 (Mount Baker Highway) to milepost 34.3, about 1 mile east of the Glacier Public Service Center. Turn right onto Glacier Creek Road (Forest Road 39) and, almost immediately, turn left onto FR 37. Follow the sign for the Skyline Divide Trail. The trailhead is 12.7 miles ahead, the last 9 of which is a gravel road that can be rough. Elevation: 4,350 feet.

The Trail

Immediately begin climbing steeply through a dense hemlock forest. Because this trail is extremely popular, use this stretch to revel in the sounds of others' heavy huffing and puffing, and remember to protect your vitals from the snouts and jaws of your fellow hikers' canines.

At about **1.0** mile the trail levels off for a short stretch, then resumes ascending and switchbacking up through an alternating mix of forest and meadow. At just over **2.0** miles, pop out of the forest for good, attain the ridge, and revel in views that are truly amazing. To the east is Mount Shuksan, that incredible rock-and-ice show-off that appears on more calendars and coffee-table books than probably any other

Mount Shuksan from Skyline Divide

mountain; to the south is Mount Baker, a big pile of snow reaching more than 2 miles high for the sky, and all around are peaks, valleys, waterfalls, wildflower meadows, and rivers that defy description—take it from me, this is a goody.

The ridge trail makes a beeline toward Mount Baker, ascending and bypassing several knolls along the way. How far you go is up to you, and because the ridge—Skyline Divide—is at about 6,000 feet, more than likely the presence of snow will play a part in your decision making. At about **3.5** miles you come to a fork.

PERMITS/CONTACT
Northwest Forest Pass required/Mount Baker–Snoqualmie National Forest, Glacier Public Service Center, (360) 599-2714

MAPS
USGS Mount Baker; Green Trails Mount Baker 13

TRAIL NOTES
Leashed dogs okay; great views

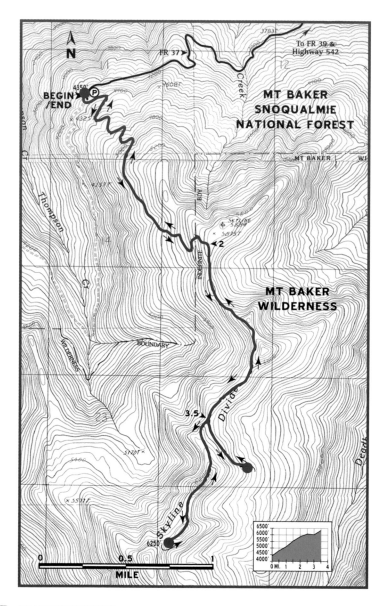

To the left: You drop down a few hundred feet over the next mile or so to talusy slopes, some more meadows, and a few rushing creeks. Return the same way.

To the right: Continue ascending along the ridge for as long as the snow level allows. The ridge trail eventually runs into Chowder Ridge, about 6 miles from the trailhead. Return the same way.

Going Farther

Boyd Creek Interpretive Trail (Hike 40) is along FR 37 about 9.4 miles from the Skyline Divide trailhead. Douglas Fir Campground is just off Highway 542 about a mile east of the turnoff onto FR 39 and FR 37. ∎

42. Horseshoe Bend Trail

RATING	DISTANCE	HIKING TIME
★★☆☆☆	2.4 miles round-trip	1 hour
ELEVATION GAIN	HIGH POINT	DIFFICULTY
350 feet	1,200 feet	◆◇◇◇◇
BEST SEASON		
Jan Feb Mar Apr May Jun Jul Aug Sep Oct Nov Dec		

The Hike

The perfect winter or rainy-day hike, Horseshoe Bend provides a lesson on the awesome power of water. Follow the raging North Fork Nooksack River as it goes head to head with boulders, snags, the riverbed, and its banks—pretty much anything in its path. Check out river kayakers, tossed about like so many fallen leaves, and in summer river rafters, doing their darnedest not to fall out.

Getting There

Head east on Highway 542 (Mount Baker Highway) to milepost 35.4, about 2 miles east of Glacier. The trailhead is on the right. Elevation: 980 feet.

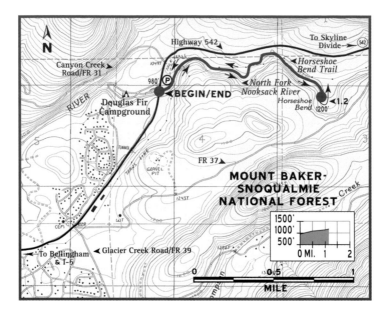

The Trail

From the roadside parking area, head down the short flight of wooden steps leading down to the river's edge. At the bottom of the steps take a left and follow the obvious trail as it parallels the rushing, gushing, at times raging North Fork Nooksack River through a gorge it finds much too narrow for its liking. This north fork of the river originates

PERMITS/CONTACT
Northwest Forest Pass required/Mount Baker–Snoqualmie National Forest,
Glacier Public Service Center, (360) 599-2714

MAPS
USGS Glacier; Green Trails Mount Baker 13

TRAIL NOTES
Leashed dogs okay; kid-friendly

A gentle forest stroll

from glaciers on Mount Shuksan's north side. Keep your eyes open for helmeted river kayakers doing that extreme thing, bouncing off boulders and weaving through snags—now you see 'em, now you don't.

A few hundred yards ahead, the trail climbs some steps and enters deeper into the dark wood. Cross a foot-drenching creek at **0.3** mile and, just ahead, a cool log bridge that, if you've brought little ones, will have you carrying them across due to its lack of railing. In a couple hundred yards, reach a spot back at the river's edge where you'll likely want to sit for hours. A well-placed bench at a bend in the river offers a front-row seat to Ragin' River, the river-rapids IMAX movie directed by Mother Nature herself. Mere feet from where you sit, the river appears to explode, most of the commotion caused by stubborn, huge gray boulders for which the river provides no impetus to move.

At about **0.7** mile, cross under a semi-open power-line area and just after, turn right onto a dirt road. In about 100 yards, rejoin the trail on the right, but not before looking up to the north for a partial view of Church Mountain. This is the closest you come on this route to an open view.

With the trail becoming more and more overgrown, return to riverside views, this time from high above. Just ahead, negotiate a steep, technical side-hill segment, the site of a past washout. A mostly dry creek bed just ahead at **1.2** miles is a good turnaround point. After this, the trail is much overgrown, and continuing on requires much head ducking and moves à la the Ministry of Silly Walks. Return the way you came.

Going Farther

From the trailhead, the Douglas Fir Campground is just across the highway. ∎

NORTH
MOUNT BAKER

---

43. Church Mountain

RATING	DISTANCE	HIKING TIME
★★★★☆	8.4 miles round-trip	6 hours
ELEVATION GAIN	**HIGH POINT**	**DIFFICULTY**
3,900 feet	6,100 feet	◆◆◆◆◇

BEST SEASON
Jan Feb Mar Apr May Jun **Jul Aug Sep Oct** Nov Dec

The Hike

South-facing Church Mountain is usually one of the first North Cascades trails to be clear of snow. But that's not all it has going for it: stupendous 360-degree mountain views and a big basin chock-full of wildflower meadows are just a couple of its other charms.

Getting There

Head east on Highway 542 (Mount Baker Highway) to milepost 38.7, about 5.5 miles east of the Glacier Public Service Center. Turn left onto gravel Church Mountain Road (Forest Road 3040) and follow it for 2.6 miles to the road-end trailhead. Elevation: 2,400 feet.

The Trail

Start by ascending the gentle grade of an old logging road for about 0.4 mile. It's a good stretch on which to loosen up for what's to come—about 2,200 feet elevation gain in less than 2 miles of steep,

PERMITS/CONTACT
Northwest Forest Pass required/Mount Baker–Snoqualmie National Forest, Glacier Public Service Center, (360) 599-2714

MAPS
USGS Bearpaw Mountain; Green Trails Mount Baker 13

TRAIL NOTES
Leashed dogs okay; great views

A classic North Cascades ridge

forested switchbacks with almost no letup. At **2.5** miles emerge from the forest and reach the expansive and open Deerhorn Creek basin. If you're wondering whether you're attempting this trail too early in the season, here's where you'll find the answer—snow lingers here longer than anywhere else on the trail.

With most of the steep stuff behind you, proceed west for about a mile, reveling in wildflowers (or snow); big-time Baker, Shuksan, and Twin Sister views; and the many creeks and creeklets offering to soak your socks. At **3.7** miles reach a fork at a mini-spur ridge, to the left is a primitive, steep, straight-up-the-gut route to the top; go to the right on the main trail, which traverses the top of a basin and, though it is more well-traveled, it can be tricky if it's muddy or there's still snow on the trail. Either way, you'll arrive at the same place—a craggy bump accessorized by the remnants of an old fire lookout.

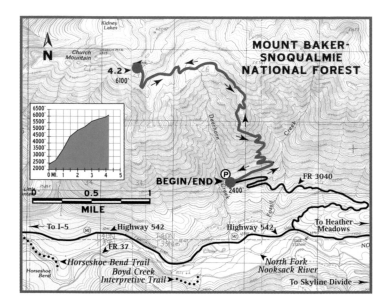

About 20 yards ahead, climb the primitive path up the rock, passing an old outhouse on the way—a true loo with a view—and at **4.2** miles attain them 360-degree mountain views.

All around you are some of the North Cascades' greatest hits— Baker, Shuksan, Tomyhoi Peak, Nooksack Ridge, the border peaks, et cetera—and, on clear days, Mount Rainier. To the immediate northwest is the true steeple of Church Mountain, a rocky pyramid that tops out about 200 feet above you and that requires a little bit of technical climbing to summit. A couple of turquoise tarns, the Kidney Lakes, are down below to the north. Return the same way.

Going Farther

From the upper reaches of Church Mountain, it's possible to follow the ridge about 10 miles to the east, partially via cross-country travel, partially on the High Divide Trail (Hike 45). See also, Damfino Lakes Trail and Excelsior Mountain (Hike 44). ∎

44. Damfino Lakes and Excelsior Mountain

RATING	DISTANCE	HIKING TIME
★★★★☆	1.8 to 6 miles round-trip	4 hours
ELEVATION GAIN	**HIGH POINT**	**DIFFICULTY**
250 feet to 1,500 feet	5,600 feet	♦♦◇◇◇

BEST SEASON
Jan Feb Mar Apr May Jun **Jul Aug Sep Oct** Nov Dec

The Hike

This gentle forest trail leads to a couple of pleasant mountain ponds offering the perfect lunch—and/or dozing—spot. Continue on to Excelsior Mountain where head-on Mount Baker views are spectacular.

Getting There

Head east on Highway 542 (Mount Baker Highway) to milepost 35.4, about 2 miles east of the Glacier Public Service Center. Turn left onto Canyon Creek Road (Forest Road 31) and follow it for 15 miles, as the winding road alternates between pavement and gravel, to the road-end parking lot. Elevation: 4,200 feet. (Note: As of press time, FR 31 was closed to motorized vehicles due to road damage. However, bicyclists and hikers are allowed past the closure. No definitive date was given for when the road will reopen.)

PERMITS/CONTACT
Northwest Forest Pass required/Mount Baker–Snoqualmie National Forest, Glacier Public Service Center, (360) 599-2714

MAPS
USGS Bearpaw Mountain; Green Trails Mount Baker 13

TRAIL NOTES
Leashed dogs okay; kid-friendly; great views

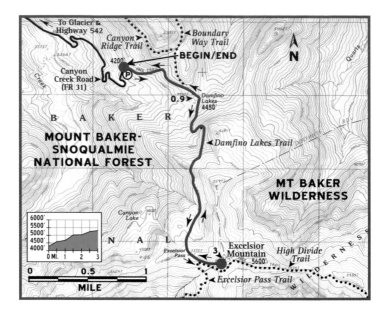

The Trail

Start with an easy forest walk—the first part a recently planted section that's home to dive-bombing hummingbirds—and at **0.7** mile
reach a signed intersection with the Canyon Ridge and Boundary
Way Trails. Go straight and in less than two shakes, drop down into
a basin and find yourself at the foot of Damfino Lakes, two peaceful,
pretty ponds. Rumor has it that in days of yore, a ranger was asked
the names of the lakes and he responded, "Damn if I know." Follow
the boardwalk around and look for a place to eat.

Excelsior Mountain: At the southeast side of the lakes, continue
following the trail as it heads back up into the trees. The trail climbs
fairly steeply, crossing at least one gusher of a creek before opening
up into a huge bowl at about **2.2** miles. In season, wildflowers are
magnifique here. The signed junction with Excelsior Pass and High
Divide Trails is straight ahead at about **2.6** miles, so make for them;

A side trip up Excelsior Mountain

you won't regret it. From the pass, Mount Baker is not a bit shy about showing off her charms.

For that "because it's there" feeling, hike about 300 feet up in about 0.4 mile to the top of the knoll to your left, Excelsior Mountain, the site of an old lookout; its 360-degree views will make you feel like you're on top of the world. Return the same way.

Going Farther

From the 0.7-mile mark on the Damfino Lakes Trail, a left leads in about 0.4 mile to the 8.7-mile (one-way) Canyon Ridge Trail that heads to the northwest, and the 3-mile (one-way) Boundary Way Trail, which heads northeast. ■

The Damfino Lakes Trail is also a popular way to access the High Divide Trail (Hike 45) which you can follow east from Excelsior Pass for 5 glorious, above-tree-line miles. From Excelsior Pass you can also take Excelsior Pass Trail (Hike 46) south, or experienced cross-country travelers can head west for about 5 miles to Church Mountain.

Douglas Fir Campground is just off the highway near the turnoff onto Canyon Creek Road (FR 31). ■

45. High Divide Trail via Damfino Lakes Trail

RATING	DISTANCE	HIKING TIME
★★★★★	14.6 miles round-trip	8 hours
ELEVATION GAIN	HIGH POINT	DIFFICULTY
3,100 feet	5,800 feet	♦♦♦♦◇
BEST SEASON		
Jan Feb Mar Apr May Jun **Jul Aug Sep Oct** Nov Dec		

The Hike
Wander a ridge-top trail through spectacular high-country meadows while peering into a million North Cascades nooks, crannies, folds, and ridges. Wildflowers and wild mountains, that's High Divide's subhead. Note: The trail description below follows the High Divide Trail from west to east, starting at Excelsior Pass and continuing to Welcome Pass. To reach Excelsior Pass, the hike follows the Damfino Lakes Trail (Hike 44).

Getting There
To reach the High Divide Trail, you must hike one of at least three trails; for the hike described here, follow Damfino Lakes and Excelsior Mountain (Hike 44), 2.6 miles to Excelsior Pass. It is also possible to follow Excelsior Pass Trail (Hike 46) to Excelsior Pass, or Welcome Pass Trail (Hike 47) to Welcome Pass and then follow the High Divide

Trail from east to west. The most popular access, and one requiring the least amount of elevation gain, is the Damfino Lakes Trail (Hike 44). However, it's the one that requires the most driving. (Note: As of press time, Forest Road 31 was closed to motorized vehicles due to road damage. However, bicyclists and hikers are allowed past the closure. No definitive date was given for when the road will reopen.)

The Trail

Follow Damfino Lakes and Excelsior Mountain (Hike 44), 2.6 miles to Excelsior Pass. From the Excelsior Pass sign, ooh and aah, ogle and eyeball some of the best straight-on, seemingly eye-level views that you'll ever have of Mount Baker. Then follow the High Divide sign that points to the trail to the east. Views from the High Divide Trail itself are just about equally as grand. Canyon Creek's valley and Bearpaw Mountain dominate the west and north (as do countless Canadian peaks); Tomyhoi Peak, Mount Larrabee, and Yellow Aster Butte (Hike 48) stand out to the east, along with Mount Shuksan and the Nooksack Ridge.

Follow the High Divide Trail as it roller-coasters gently along the ridge, bisecting meadows wild with paintbrush, daisies, lupines, and blueberries; cross through brief stands of some of the heartiest timber anywhere. Mostly though, bask in the glorious alpine scenery—it surrounds you on all sides. In about 1.4 miles reach the high point at **4.0** miles, and follow this ridgeline about 0.25 mile, then switchback about 300 feet down to about **4.6** miles.

PERMITS/CONTACT
Northwest Forest Pass required/Mount Baker–Snoqualmie National Forest, Glacier Public Service Center, (360) 599-2714

MAPS
USGS Mount Larrabee; Green Trails, Mount Baker 13, Mount Shuksan 14

TRAIL NOTES
Leashed dogs okay; great views

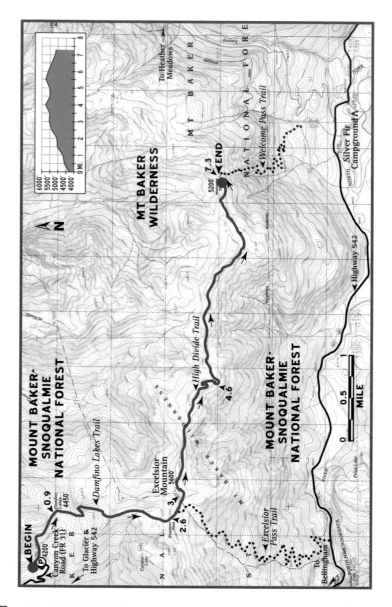

The trail continues to roller-coaster another 2.75 miles. At **7.3** miles, reach Welcome Pass, where that trail, Hike 47, leads to the right and into the forest. Turn around here and return as you came.

Going Farther

For a 9.8-mile one-way hike that includes the best of the Damfino Lakes, Excelsior Pass, High Divide, and Welcome Pass areas, hike the Damfino Lakes Trail (Hike 44) to Excelsior Pass, then the High Divide Trail west to east, then the Welcome Pass Trail (Hike 47), and prearrange to have transportation meet you at the Welcome Pass trailhead. A similar one-way hike could be done following the Excelsior Pass Trail (Hike 46) rather than the Damfino Lakes Trail, for 11.4 miles one-way (and trailheads that are a bit closer together).

For nearby camping options, see the three trails that provide access to the High Divide Trail (Hike 45), Damfino Lakes and Excelsior Mountain (Hike 44), Excelsior Pass Trail (Hike 46), and Welcome Pass (Hike 47). ∎

46. Excelsior Pass Trail

RATING	DISTANCE	HIKING TIME
★★★☆☆	**9.2 miles round-trip**	**6 hours**
ELEVATION GAIN	HIGH POINT	DIFFICULTY
3,900 feet	**5,700 feet**	◆◆◆◆◇
BEST SEASON		
Jan Feb Mar Apr May Jun **Jul Aug Sep Oct** Nov Dec		

The Hike

After steep, seemingly endless switchbacks through heavy timber, this trail rewards with entry into a magical land of mountains and meadows, flowers and berries. Advantages (besides ridgetop views): access is easy-right off the Mount Baker Highway. Disadvantages: steep, seemingly endless switchbacks through heavy timber and . . . there is an easier, more pleasant way to get here; see

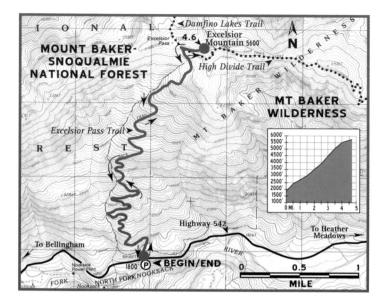

Damfino Lakes and Excelsior Mountain (Hike 44)—however, that way requires a lot more driving.

Getting There

Head east on Highway 542 (Mount Baker Highway) to milepost 41.2, about 8 miles east of the Glacier Public Service Center. Park

---

PERMITS/CONTACT
Northwest Forest Pass required/Mount Baker–Snoqualmie National Forest, Glacier Public Service Center, (360) 599-2714

MAPS
USGS Bearpaw Mountain; Green Trails Mount Baker 13

TRAIL NOTES
Leashed dogs okay; great views

Mount Baker from Excelsior Pass

in the large parking lot on the north (left) side of the road. Elevation: 1,800 feet.

The Trail

Upon entering the deep forest, the trail follows an old logging road for a short stretch, then begins climbing (and switchbacking) in earnest. The sound of forest silence replaces the sound of the rushing

North Fork Nooksack River, and now it's just you, your thoughts, and the trees. Peace—and huffing and puffing—abounds. Pass through a stretch of forest logged early last century as well as a section that burned and is now in the process of repopulating the hill. At several points, the trail approaches but never quite crosses a rushing stream. It's a nice water source and also offers a couple of impressive waterfalls.

At about **1.6** miles, the trail becomes rockier, more root-strewn, and, in general, rougher. This trail is popular with equestrians and shows the signs in more ways than one. Watch your step. In more ways than one. After about 2 more miles, pop out of the forest onto the meadowed southern slope of Excelsior Ridge. Cross a creek, switchback once or twice more, and at **4.2** miles reach Excelsior Pass and the junction with the High Divide Trail (Hike 45). Turn around to the south and gape—Mount Baker, crevassed glaciers and all, is almost too big to be believed. Mountain, meadow, and valley views are to be had in all directions—your Bearpaw Mountain, your Tomyhoi Peak, your Shuksan, your British Columbia, and more.

If you're up for it, scramble about 0.4 mile and 300 feet up to the top of the nubbin just to the east. The 360-degree views from atop Excelsior Mountain, the site of a former lookout, are the perfect lunch accompaniment. Return the same way.

Going Farther

The High Divide Trail (Hike 45) continues east from Excelsior Pass for 4.7 miles to Welcome Pass. The Damfino Lakes Trail (Hike 44) continues north from Excelsior Pass for 2.6 miles. ∎

47. Welcome Pass

RATING	DISTANCE	HIKING TIME
★★★☆☆	**5 miles round-trip**	**5 hours**

ELEVATION GAIN	HIGH POINT	DIFFICULTY
3,000 feet	**5,200 feet**	♦♦♦♦♦

BEST SEASON		
Jan Feb Mar Apr May Jun **Jul Aug Sep Oct** Nov Dec		

The Hike

Short but steep—more than 1,000 feet of elevation gain per mile, most of it in heavy timber. Then why hike it? Because the aptly named Welcome Pass greets you with bee-buzzin' wildflower meadows and airplane-wing views of the North Cascades all-star team—Baker, Shuksan, Larrabee, American Border Peak, et cetera. This trail also accesses the High Divide Trail (Hike 45), a magical ridgeline trail that you'll never want to leave.

Getting There

Head east on Highway 542 (Mount Baker Highway) to milepost 45.9, about 12.5 miles east of the Glacier Public Service Center. Turn left onto Forest Road 3060, an easy-to-miss primitive dirt road, and follow it for about 0.75 mile to the road-end trailhead. Elevation: 2,450 feet.

The Trail

The trail starts out innocently enough, following an old logging road that's not overly eager to leave the North Fork Nooksack River valley. At about **1.0** mile you've gained only a couple hundred feet, but now the fun starts—if "fun" means short, steep, ping-ponging switch-backs. (It's said that there are sixty-seven of them.)

You get up the mountain in a hurry, climbing about 2,200 feet in 1.5 miles. Dense forest means you won't be distracted from your task, either. Ah, but at **2.5** miles reach the pass and say hello to wide-open meadows, ridges, buttes, valleys, and British Columbia, less than 5 air miles away. Return the same way.

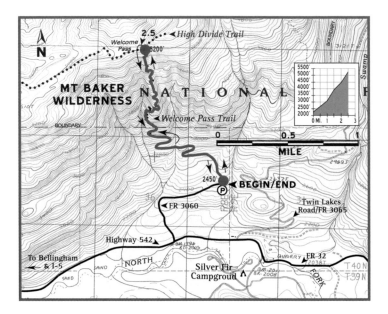

Going Farther

From Welcome Pass, continue about 0.25 mile either to the right or the left for full-on 360-degree Baker-'n'-Shuksan-'n'-Larrabee-'n'-Tomyhoi views that'll make your socks drop, if they don't knock 'em right off. The trail to the left, the High Divide Trail (Hike 45) continues west for

---

PERMITS/CONTACT
None required/Mount Baker–Snoqualmie National Forest, Glacier Public Service Center, (360) 599-2714

MAPS
USGS Mount Larrabee; Green Trails Mount Shuksan 14

TRAIL NOTES
Leashed dogs okay; great views

about 5 miles to Excelsior Pass. See the Going Farther section for Hike 45 for descriptions of various options for this truly grand traverse.

Camping is available at Silver Fir Campground just off Highway 542 about 0.8 mile east of the FR 3060 turnoff. ■

48. Yellow Aster Butte

RATING	DISTANCE	HIKING TIME
★ ★ ★ ★ ★	7 miles round-trip	4 hours
ELEVATION GAIN	**HIGH POINT**	**DIFFICULTY**
2,550 feet	6,145 feet	♦ ♦ ♦ ♦

BEST SEASON
Jan Feb Mar Apr May Jun **Jul Aug Sep Oct** Nov Dec

The Hike

They ain't yellow asters—they're daisies—but what's in a trail name anyway? This trail, by any name, is just grand and features a number of neat places to explore—ponds 'n' tarns 'n' old mining equipment. And the 360-degree alpine views from the butte (yes, it really is a butte) are seriously terrif.

Getting There

Head east on Highway 542 (Mount Baker Highway) to milepost 46.3, about 13 miles east of the Glacier Public Service Center. Turn left onto gravel Twin Lakes Road (Forest Road 3065) and follow it for 4.5 miles to the trailhead. Elevation: 3,600 feet.

The Trail

After craning your neck in giving towering Goat Mountain a good once- or twice-over gawk, begin a steep climb on good trail that at first can't make up its mind whether it's a forest or a meadow hike. Soon enough, it settles on dense forest while keeping up the steepness. At about **1.5** miles, break out of the woods and enter a meadowy bowl.

A steel curtain sky over Mount Shuksan

Just ahead at a fork, go left following the sign for Yellow Aster Butte, which is visible on high to the west.

Continue a mostly level and open traverse around the inside of the bowl—Baker, Shuksan, and Goat Mountain views pulling you along—and pass through a rocky, boulder-strewn stretch about 0.5 mile farther. Snow lingers fairly long in this haven for hoary marmots, so follow cairns and/or boot track if you have to. Or turn around if you're unsure where to pick up the trail.

Resume more meadow traversing behavior—wildflowers along with increasingly stunning alpine views yanking you onward—and at about **2.7** miles, maneuver a short, steep stretch and soon find yourself

PERMITS/CONTACT
Northwest Forest Pass required/Mount Baker–Snoqualmie National Forest, Glacier Public Service Center, (360) 599-2714

MAPS
USGS Mount Larrabee; Green Trails Mount Shuksan 14

TRAIL NOTES
Leashed dogs okay; great views

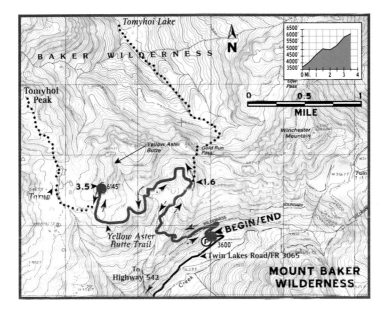

heading almost due west. High Divide, a 10-plus–mile ridgeful of fun, is visible. Round a bend to head north and see Tomyhoi Peak, high above and across the tarn-spattered valley that separates you. At a fork in the trail, you have the option of going left and dropping down and visiting that magical land o' lakes where time seems to stand still. Remnants of old mining equipment recall sourdoughs in days of yore trying to scrape a living out of these here hills.

Take a right to head for the top of Yellow Aster Butte at **3.5** miles. It's a steep 600 feet—the trail was blazed by someone who no doubt thought that switchbacks are for sissies—but it's not that long and once you're on top, you'll soon forget the huffin' and a-puffin' you did to get there. You're surrounded by a sea of peaks—the aforementioned all-stars to the south and east; Mount Larrabee, the border peaks, and a ton of Canadian crags to the north; Church, Bearpaw, and others to the west. Return the same way.

Going Farther

To go to Gold Run Pass and Tomyhoi Lake, at the fork at 1.6 miles, continue straight. The lake is about 5 miles (one-way) from the trailhead.

Tomyhoi Peak is a popular climb that's accessed via the Yellow Aster Butte Trail. Follow the trail to the fork near 2.7 miles, and take the left trail as though you were going to hike to the tarns. Follow a climbers' trail that heads about 2.5 miles north to the peak. The climb is not supertechnical, though rock-climbing experience is advised and most who climb it do use a rope.

Campsites are available near the tarns about 0.75 mile west of Yellow Aster Butte, at Twin Lakes another 2.5 miles up FR 3065 from the trailhead, and at Silver Fir Campground on Highway 542 about 0.5 mile east of the turnoff for FR 3065. ■

49. Winchester Mountain Lookout

RATING	DISTANCE	HIKING TIME
★★★★☆	3.2 miles round-trip	2 hours
ELEVATION GAIN	HIGH POINT	DIFFICULTY
1,350 feet	6,510 feet	◆◆◇◇◇

BEST SEASON
Jan Feb Mar Apr May Jun **Jul Aug Sep Oct** Nov Dec

The Hike

Perhaps no other Mount Baker Highway–accessed trail makes you feel so much as though you're smack in the middle of the mountains with such tiny effort. Plus, Winchester's spiff summit sports an old fire lookout, maintained by the Mount Baker Hiking Club. In a perfect setting such as this—the peaceful, mile-high Twin Lakes mirroring countless peaks make them seem twice as countless—you may not feel the need to hike. But do it anyway. The trail to Winchester Mountain's lookout is short but very sweet.

Getting There

Head east on Highway 542 (Mount Baker Highway) to milepost 46.3, about 13 miles east of the Glacier Public Service Center. Turn left onto gravel Twin Lakes Road (Forest Road 3065) and follow it for 7 miles. Note: The last 2.5 miles of this road are extremely rough. (If you don't have a bomber SUV-type vehicle or you don't want a jarring ride that's going to loosen your dental work, consider parking at the Yellow Aster Butte trailhead at 4.5 miles, elevation 3,600 feet, and hiking the road the last 2.5 miles to the trailhead, an elevation gain of 1,550 feet.) The Winchester Mountain trailhead is between the Twin Lakes. Elevation: 5,200 feet.

The Trail

After looking high up Winchester Mountain to the west to see if you can spot the lookout, follow the obvious trail as it gradually switchbacks up a mix of wildflower meadows and hearty trees. In about **0.25** mile, at a signed intersection with the trail to High Pass, continue straight. Climb gradually, up mostly open meadow and just go "Wowza!" at the views, which, though it doesn't seem possible, only get better with each step. Just across the Swamp Creek valley to the south, Goat Mountain does its darnedest to steal focus from mammoth Mounts Shuksan and Baker.

At about **1.4** miles reach a shoulder offering views to the west that include Yellow Aster Butte and Tomyhoi Peak, which appears to be dipping its toes in Tomyhoi Lake. Winchester's lookout-crowned summit and its 360-degree views of mountains both near and far—really

---

PERMITS/CONTACT
Northwest Forest Pass required/Mount Baker–Snoqualmie National Forest, Glacier Public Service Center, (360) 599-2714

MAPS
USGS Mount Larrabee; Green Trails Mount Shuksan 14

TRAIL NOTES
Leashed dogs okay; kid-friendly; great views

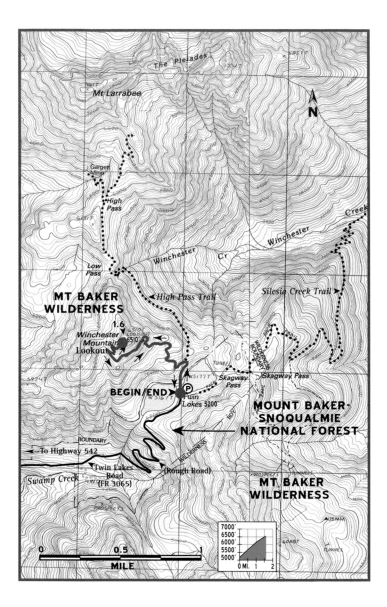

The Pleiades

Mt Larrabee

N

Gargett
Mine

High
Pass

Low
Pass

Winchester Cr

Winchester Creek

Silesia Creek Trail ▶

High Pass Trail

MT BAKER
WILDERNESS

1.6

Winchester
Mountain
Lookout

6510

WILDERNESS BOUNDARY

TUNNEL

Skagway
Pass

Skagway Pass

BEGIN/END ▶

P

Twin
Lakes 5200'

WILDERNESS

MOUNT BAKER-
SNOQUALMIE
NATIONAL FOREST

BOUNDARY

◀ To Highway 542

Twin Lakes
Road
[FR 3065]

(Rough Road)

Swamp Creek

PROSPECTS

MT BAKER
WILDERNESS

USMM

0   0.5   1

MILE

7000'
6500'
6000'
5500'
5000'

0 MI. 1   2

far—is just 0.2 mile above. From there, row upon row of snowy and/or rocky peaks extend in all directions. Rusty Mount Larrabee is directly north, backed by American Border Peak, just inside the US-Canada border about 3 miles away. Check out the Pickets to the south, far beyond Baker and various ridges, passes, divides, and valleys to the west. Also notable are the . . . ahem, Big Bosom Buttes, the nearby if sophomorically named peaks just to the east, their tips reflecting in the Twin Lakes below.

Going Farther

The High Pass Trail (Hike 50) leaves from the same trailhead as the Winchester Mountain Trail. Both are short enough to do in one day or on separate days if you're camping nearby.

The 6.5-mile (one-way) Silesia Creek Trail heads northeast from Twin Lakes. This heavily wooded trail loses about 2,800 feet and tends to be overgrown at times.

Camping is available at Twin Lakes and at Silver Fir Campground on Highway 542 about 0.5 mile east of the turnoff for FR 3065. ■

50. High Pass Trail

RATING	DISTANCE	HIKING TIME
★★★★☆	**4 miles round-trip**	**3 hours**
ELEVATION GAIN	HIGH POINT	DIFFICULTY
1,400 feet	**6,000 feet**	♦♦◇◇◇
BEST SEASON		
Jan Feb Mar Apr May Jun **Jul Aug Sep Oct** Nov Dec		

The Hike

Less well-traveled than the Winchester Mountain Trail (Hike 49), High Pass Trail delights with nearly comparable alpine scenery and perhaps a superior blueberry-'n'-wildflowers quotient. Hike to the foot of russet-sloped Mount Larrabee; when snow-covered, this

Mini-Everest from High Pass

pyramidal peak resembles a mini-Everest. Really mini. Take photos and trick your friends.

Getting There

Head east on Highway 542 (Mount Baker Highway) to milepost 46.3, about 13 miles east of the Glacier Public Service Center. Turn left onto gravel Twin Lakes Road (Forest Road 3065) and follow it for 7 miles.

PERMITS/CONTACT
Northwest Forest Pass required/Mount Baker–Snoqualmie National Forest, Glacier Public Service Center, (360) 599-2714

MAPS
USGS Mount Larrabee; Green Trails Mount Shuksan 14

TRAIL NOTES
Leashed dogs okay; kid-friendly; great views

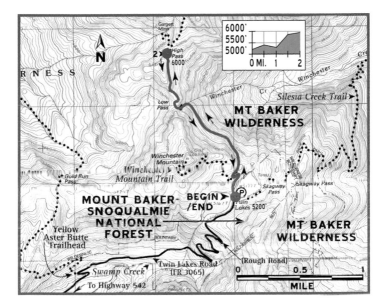

Note: The last 2.5 miles of this road are extremely rough. (If you don't have a bomber SUV-type vehicle or you don't want a jarring ride that's going to loosen your dental work, consider parking at the Yellow Aster Butte trailhead at 4.5 miles, elevation 3,600 feet, and hiking the road the last 2.5 miles, an elevation gain of 1,600 feet.) The High Pass trailhead is between the Twin Lakes. Elevation: 5,200 feet.

The Trail

From Twin Lakes, follow the obvious meadow-climbing trail that also leads to Winchester Mountain (Hike 49). After about 0.25 mile, at a signed intersection with the trail to Winchester Mountain, go right, following the sign for High Pass. Continue climbing for a couple hundred yards until you reach a saddle. Grand views open to the north, in particular stunning Mount Larrabee flanked by the craggy-topped Pleiades to the east. Follow the trail as it drops down the saddle's north slope, losing more than 300 feet in no time.

After leveling off, the trail makes a beeline for Mount Larrabee, traversing a meadowed slope where in high summer the Indian paintbrush are so abundant that you almost expect your legs to be splashed crimson. At **1.0** mile, begin a short, steep series of switchbacks up a talus slope, at the top of which you find yourself at Low Pass, High Pass's cousin. Catch views to the west of the Yellow Aster Butte–Tomyhoi Peak end of the world, which go nicely with the sea of British Columbian peaks to the northeast. Winchester Mountain is at your back.

Over the next mile, alternate between short, steep stretches and a gentle, forested traverse. At **2.0** miles reach High Pass. Larrabee is a stone's throw away. Return as you came. High Pass is in high country where snow often lingers into August.

Going Farther

From High Pass, the somewhat primitive trail to the right heads up steeply (700 feet) for 0.6 mile, and almost always requires some snow travel. Another fun exploratory trail from High Pass heads west 0.4 mile across Larrabee's flank and down 400 feet to the old Gargett Mine, complete with rusty, twisted mining equipment.

The Winchester Mountain Trail (Hike 49) leaves from the same trailhead as the High Pass Trail. Both are short enough to do in one day or on separate days if you're camping nearby.

The 6.5-mile (one-way) Silesia Creek Trail heads northeast from Twin Lakes. This heavily wooded trail loses about 2,800 feet and tends to be overgrown at times.

Camping is available at Twin Lakes and at Silver Fir Campground on Highway 542 about 0.5 mile east of the turnoff for FR 3065. ■

51. Goat Mountain

RATING	DISTANCE	HIKING TIME
★ ★ ★ ★ ★	**11 miles round-trip**	**7 hours**
ELEVATION GAIN	HIGH POINT	DIFFICULTY
4,200 feet	**6,550 feet**	◆ ◆ ◆ ◆ ◇
BEST SEASON		
Jan Feb Mar Apr May Jun **Jul Aug Sep Oct** Nov Dec		

The Hike

Often overlooked by those looking for Mount Baker–area hikes, Goat Mountain is an underrated gem. Sure, it involves some hard work—4,200 feet of elevation gain if you're heading all the way up—but what's a little climbing when the views are this good? Hike to the top for 360-degree mountain, meadow, and river valley views. Because it's south-facing, this is one of the first opportunities to get high (in the mountains).

Getting There

Head east on Highway 542 (Mount Baker Highway) to milepost 46.5, turn left on Hannegan Pass Road (Forest Road 32), and continue for about 1.3 miles to a fork. Bear left to stay on FR 32, and reach the easy-to-miss pullout parking area in another 1.2 miles. Elevation 2,500 feet.

PERMITS/CONTACT
Northwest Forest Pass required/Mount Baker–Snoqualmie National Forest, Glacier Public Service Center, (360) 599-2714

MAPS
USGS Mount Larrabee; Green Trails Mount Shuksan 14

TRAIL NOTES
Leashed dogs okay; kid-friendly; great views

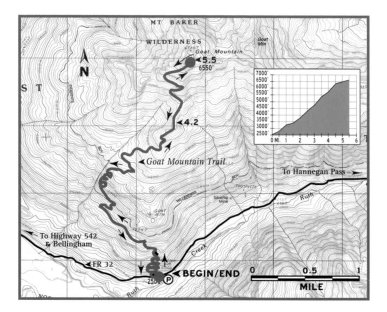

The Trail

Start by switchbacking up through dense, shut-out-the-sky forest, gaining about 800 feet over the first mile. Marvel at the number of fire-scarred trees still standing after blazes that burned more than forty years ago.

At about **1.8** miles, pass under the sign hailing your entry into the Mount Baker Wilderness. A couple hundred yards ahead, an obscure and overgrown trail to the right leads about half a mile to the site of an old lookout cabin. On the main trail, resume climbing and switchbacking in earnest as the trail narrows but remains easy to follow.

At about **2.8** miles, enjoy the first views south across the North Fork Nooksack River valley. See regal and icy Mount Shuksan, the Heather Meadows area, flat-top Table Mountain, and just the tippy top of a coy Mount Baker. In about a mile, the trail enters a damp, heathery stretch with several steep, muddy gullies leading the way. Pick the one that seems least damaging—to you and the surrounding vegetation—and

Rewarding views from the flank of Goat Mountain

continue. But first, look north and about 1,000 feet up at the upper reaches of Goat Mountain—in not too long, you'll be there.

Soon enter a flat, semi-open stretch that makes for a perfect picnic/turnaround spot at about **4.2** miles. Views here are simply superb—Mount Sefrit, the western bookend of the Nooksack Ridge, dominates the foreground with Mounts Shuksan, Baker, et alia, beyond. Check out remote Price Lake, imbibing from the meltwater of Shuksan's Price Glacier and appearing close enough that you could skip stones across it.

After some oohs and aahs, perhaps yummies for tummies, find the primitive trail that continues north and up. From here the trail is prone to being overgrown and can be hard to follow, especially if there are still snow patches. The trail follows minor ridges, passes through the few trees hanging on for life at this elevation, and begins switch-backing up a large meadow. Then suddenly the trail—while heading west—seems to stop just before a creek. No explanation, just no more trail. Turn around and, facing east, look up. You should be able to find the ever more-primitive trail as it continues climbing the meadow.

Tomyhoi Peak and its broad shoulders

From here on up, it's steep side-hill action with a few talus slopes, slippery dirt/mud, and creek crossings to negotiate. Finally, at about **5.0** miles, reach a way-high ridge that offers stupendous views north and west. Follow the obvious ridgeline, above-tree-line trail to the nontechnical rock summit that delivers out-of-this-world 360-degree views. (A much more technical summit is just to the north, but no biggie—it's not that much higher than where you are.) Your Tomyhoi Peak, your Mount Larrabee, your Skagit and Nooksack Ridges—along with Mounts Shuksan and Baker and seemingly all of lower British Columbia—appear close enough to touch. Return the same way.

Going Farther
Camping is available at the Silver Fir Campground, near the intersection of Hannegan Pass Road (FR 32) and Highway 542. ■

52. Hannegan Pass and Peak

RATING	DISTANCE	HIKING TIME
★★★★★	8 to 10.4 miles round-trip	4 to 6 hours

ELEVATION GAIN	HIGH POINT	DIFFICULTY
3,100 feet to 2,000 feet	6,187 feet	◆◆◆◆◇

BEST SEASON
Jan Feb Mar Apr May Jun **Jul Aug Sep Oct** Nov Dec

The Hike

It's nice that the Hannegan Pass Trail takes its time easing into the high country because there's much to see: waterfalls spilling down the Nooksack Ridge, icy Ruth Mountain rising before your eyes, raging Ruth Creek snaking through the valley below. Meanwhile, the Hannegan Peak Trail, an express route to the roof of the North Cascades, climbs more than 1,000 feet in about a mile.

Getting There

Head east on Highway 542 (Mount Baker Highway) to milepost 46.5, turn left on Hannegan Pass Road (Forest Road 32), and continue for about 1.3 miles to a fork. Bear left to continue on FR 32 and reach the road-end parking lot in another 4 miles. Elevation 3,100 feet.

The Trail

This trail—one of the first of the Mount Baker Highway–accessed mountain trails to be free of snow—gains almost no elevation at first, allowing you to get good and loose for the steeper climbs to come. Thing is, by that time you're on such a mountain high that the ascent doesn't seem so bad. Start by climbing very gradually, some in forest, some in open meadow, which, along with wildflower ogling, allows views of the towering Nooksack Ridge high above and Ruth Creek below.

Cross several creeks, being careful as you do—in June and July, they're likely covered by snowbridges in various stage of melt; in August and September, they're likely to be raging. Or dry as a bone.

Mountain peaks from Hannegan Peak

While the trail has gotten gradually steeper throughout, at about **3.2** miles it begins doing so in earnest as it switchbacks through forest. You'll gain 600 feet in elevation over the next 0.8-mile homestretch to Hannegan Pass. About halfway up, where the sign for Hannegan Camp urges you to the right, bear left. (I've personally never seen bears at Hannegan Camp, but I've often heard about brazen members of the ursine persuasion making nuisances of themselves near there.)

At **4.0** miles reach signed Hannegan Pass, a hub for various backpacking and climbing routes in North Cascades National Park. It's a great place for lunch or to turn around, but because it's forested,

PERMITS/CONTACT
Northwest Forest Pass required/Mount Baker–Snoqualmie National Forest, Glacier Public Service Center, (360) 599-2714

MAPS
USGS Mount Sefrit; Green Trails Mount Shuksan 14

TRAIL NOTES
Leashed dogs okay; kid-friendly; great views

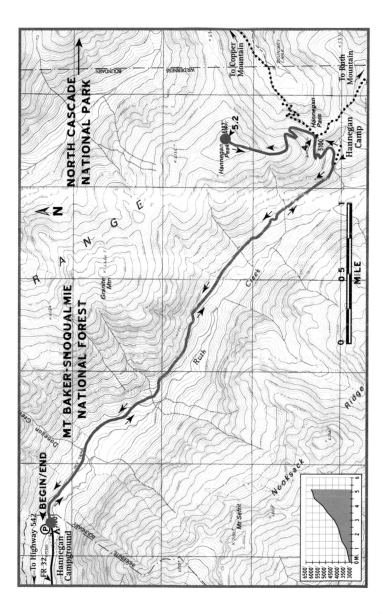

Ruth Mountain and Mount Shuksan

the views here aren't quite as inspiring as they are from the top of Hannegan Peak, just 1.2 miles away. And 1,100 feet above. If you're up for it, go left to follow the signed Hannegan Peak Trail just north of the pass and begin fighting gravity almost immediately.

Views improve exponentially of sights both near—a massive wildflower meadow—and far: Mounts Shuksan and Baker along with Ruth Mountain, form an amazing triumvirate of ice, rock, and snow. At **5.2** miles, reach the peak and spin around—glorious mountains are everywhere! Short, scrubby trees at the summit block the wind, making it a perfect munch spot. Return the same way.

Going Farther

From Hannegan Pass the trail to Copper Mountain is straight ahead, heading east about 6 miles. The trail to the right at Hannegan Pass leads south to Ruth Mountain about 2 miles. Follow it for a short while for better views than at Hannegan Pass, but because Ruth Mountain is glaciated, this trail eventually becomes quite technical. Proper equipment and glacier travel experience is required.

Camping is available at Hannegan Campground at the trailhead and at Hannegan Camp, about 0.5 mile before Hannegan Pass. You can also camp at Hannegan Peak's summit. ■

HEATHER MEADOWS

53. Picture Lake

RATING	DISTANCE	HIKING TIME
★★★ ☆☆	0.5-mile loop	30 minutes

ELEVATION GAIN	HIGH POINT	DIFFICULTY
None	4,100 feet	◆ ◇ ◇ ◇ ◇

BEST SEASON
Jan Feb Mar Apr May Jun Jul Aug Sep Oct Nov Dec

The Hike

This is not really a hike so much as a paved path through an alpine wonderland. Ever seen a postcard photo of Mount Shuksan and its brilliant reflection in an alpine lake, the heathered banks of which are a kaleidoscope of fall colors? Here's where it was taken. And why September and October are the best months to visit. Easy access means you won't be lonely.

Getting There

Head east on Highway 542 (Mount Baker Highway) to milepost 54.1, about 21 miles east of the Glacier Public Service Center. The lake is just below the Mount Baker Ski Area's upper lodge. Elevation: 4,100 feet.

The Trail

From the trailhead kiosk follow the paved-and-boardwalk path as it circles Picture Lake. Expect crowds, blueberries in late summer,

---

PERMITS/CONTACT
Northwest Forest Pass required/Mount Baker–Snoqualmie National Forest, Glacier Public Service Center, (360) 599-2714

MAPS
USGS Shuksan Arm; Green Trails Mount Shuksan 14

TRAIL NOTES
Kid-friendly; great views; wheelchair-accessible

Required photograph for Northwesterners

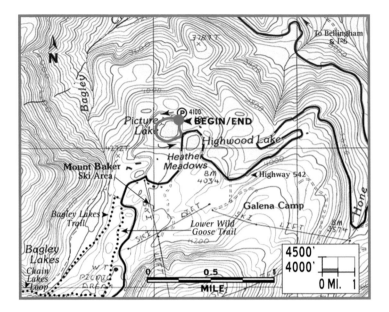

wildflowers, heather that appears aflame in fall, the music of multiple languages being spoken (a function of the aforementioned crowds), picnic benches and a mini-dock for deep-down stares into the lake, and, of course, stunning Mount Shuksan, always to the east and always ready for its close-up, Mr. DeMille.

Several spurs veer off the main loop, offering the chance for further exploration. Mount Herman and flat-top Table Mountain rise above to the west, and to Shuksan's left, take note of oft-ignored Ruth Mountain, a feisty 7,000-footer in her own right. Then go ahead; click away at Shuksan and its reflection in the lake. (Actually, to reach the best place to shoot the photo, follow the trail to the east end of the lake, cross the road, and use Highwood Lake, an adjacent pond, as the reflecting body of water.)

Going Farther

In winter and early spring, this whole area becomes a snow-filled basin great for sledding, tubing, and all-around snow sliding. In hiking season, nearby is the trailhead for Bagley Lakes and Lower Wild Goose Trails (Hike 54); just up the road is the trailhead for Chain Lakes (Hike 55), Upper Wild Goose, and Fire and Ice Trails; farther up the road is the Lake Ann trailhead (Hike 56); and at road's end is the trailhead for Table Mountain (Hike 58), Ptarmigan Ridge (Hike 59), and Artist Ridge Trail (Hike 57). ■

54. Bagley Lakes–Lower Wild Goose Trails Loop

RATING	DISTANCE	HIKING TIME
★★★ ☆ ☆	1.5-mile loop	1 hour
ELEVATION GAIN	HIGH POINT	DIFFICULTY
150 feet	4,400 feet	♦ ◆ ◆ ◆ ◆
BEST SEASON		
Jan Feb Mar Apr May Jun **Jul Aug Sep Oct** Nov Dec		

The Hike

This gentle creek- and lakeside jaunt threads its way through a heathery meadow- and rock-strewn canyon on its way to the big basin below Table Mountain. What're those columns of rock everywhere? Andesite, and you'll agree they're outta sight. (Snow lingers long into summer in this valley. Check with the ranger for the latest conditions.)

Getting There

Head east on Highway 542 (Mount Baker Highway) to milepost 55 and the overflow parking lot for the Mount Baker Ski Area's upper lodge, about 22 miles east of the Glacier Public Service Center. Find the sign for the Bagley Lakes trailhead. Elevation: 4,250 feet.

Lakes leading to Table Mountain

The Trail

From the parking lot follow the sign for Bagley Lakes and go right, dropping down quickly into a narrow gorge. At the lower bridge to the Chain Lakes Loop (in summer 2001, the bridge was under repair), follow the signed trail to the left and make for Table Mountain's mighty prow at the far south end of the canyon. Lower Bagley Lake is on your right, as is impressive, if somewhat unsung Mount Herman, above.

PERMITS/CONTACT
Northwest Forest Pass required/Mount Baker–Snoqualmie National Forest, Glacier Public Service Center, (360) 599-2714

MAPS
USGS Shuksan Arm; Green Trails Mount Shuksan 14

TRAIL NOTES
Leashed dogs okay; kid-friendly; great views

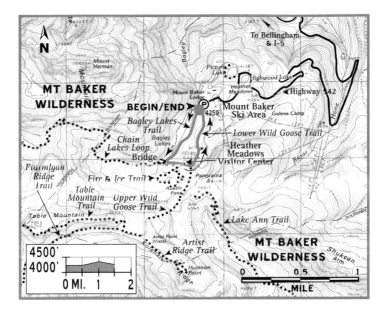

Along with summer wildflowers, late-summer blueberries, and autumn reds and yellows, water is in plentiful supply here as is its cousin, mud. Watch your footing. Shortly after oohing and aahing at rushing Bagley Creek blasting its way through a boulder-choked stretch, reach an arched stone bridge at **0.7** mile and rather than cross it, go left—a right leads once again to the Chain Lakes Loop (Hike 55). Check out upper Bagley Lake at the bottom of Table Mountain's big basin, where there's always snow and one sort of critter or another— marmot, snowboarder, telemark skier—sliding down it.

Climb steeply up one of several trails that all lead to the same place, the Heather Meadows Visitors Center. The rock here is especially beautiful; one of the trails maneuvers atop a stretch that's like a giant tortoise shell. In the picnic area just beyond the visitors center, find a sign for the Wild Goose Trail and head to the left (north). Several trails snake through this meadow and forested area and they all eventually lead down to the Wild Goose Trail. Views north include the whole Tomyhoi Peak–Mount Larrabee–Goat Mountain–Nooksack Ridge gang. Complete the loop back to the parking lot at **1.5** miles.

Going Farther

From the Heather Meadows Visitors Center, the 0.5-mile Fire and Ice Trail loop winds through meadows interspersed with way-old hemlocks that don't show their age—they're not that tall—because their growing season is so short. About half of the trail is paved and the rest is barrier-free. Interpretive signs along the way fill you in on the flora, fauna, and landscape.

The upper portion of the Wild Goose Trail also leaves from the visitors center and heads south (and way up) to Artist Point. In about 0.75 mile, the trail climbs about 600 feet and almost always requires some snow crossing.

Down the road a way is the Picture Lake loop (Hike 53); a short way up the road is the Lake Ann trailhead (Hike 56); and at road's end is the trailhead for Table Mountain (Hike 58), Ptarmigan Ridge (Hike 59), and Artist Ridge Trail (Hike 57). ■

55. Chain Lakes Loop

RATING	DISTANCE	HIKING TIME
★★★★★	6-mile loop	4 hours
ELEVATION GAIN	**HIGH POINT**	**DIFFICULTY**
1,850 feet	5,400 feet	♦♦◇◇◇
BEST SEASON		
Jan Feb Mar Apr May Jun **Jul Aug Sep Oct** Nov Dec		

The Hike

Because they offer surprises with almost every step, loop trails are aces, and the Chain Lakes Loop delights in spades. Mega-sized views of Mounts Baker and Shuksan as well as close-up ones of Table Mountain combine with peaceful ponds and blueberry meadows

Lakes along the loop

to make for a truly wonderful hike. On summer weekends there are mega-crowds at the trailhead, but they're not so bad near the lakes.

Note. One can start this trail from either the Heather Meadows Visitors Center or at road's end at Artist Point. The trail description below is from the visitors center, which starts out with a steep climb that gains 600 feet over the first 0.8 mile. (If you start at Artist Point, you finish with that steep climb.)

PERMITS/CONTACT
Northwest Forest Pass required/Mount Baker–Snoqualmie National Forest, Glacier Public Service Center, (360) 599-2714

MAPS
USGS Shuksan Arm; Green Trails Mount Shuksan 14

TRAIL NOTES
Leashed dogs okay; great views

Iceberg Lake and Table Mountain

Getting There

Head east on Highway 542 (Mount Baker Highway) almost as far as the road goes (about 55 miles, 22 miles east of Glacier), to the Heather Meadows Visitor Center, about 0.75 mile past the Mount Baker Ski Area's upper lodge. Park in the ample parking lots. Elevation: 4,400 feet. (To start and finish at Artist Point, continue on Highway 542 another 3 miles to the road-end Artist Point parking lot, elevation 5,100 feet.)

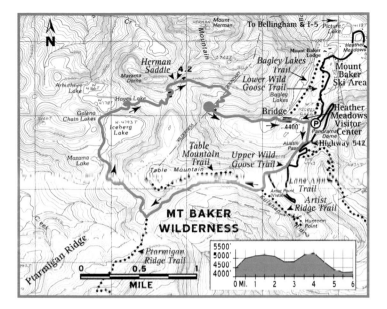

The Trail

Start on the signed Upper Wild Goose Trail at the south end of the upper parking lot. Start climbing immediately. The trail heads for Artist Point and parallels the road part of the way. Check out flat-topped Table Mountain up ahead, broken-topped Mount Shuksan to the left, and Bagley Lakes below and to the right. Herman Saddle, high above the lakes, is where you'll emerge in a few hours.

At about **0.8** mile, reach the Artist Point parking lot. Watching out for buses and cars, cross the lot and follow the sign for Chain Lakes Loop. Stay to the left—don't head right and up toward the top of Table Mountain—and soon begin a mostly level traverse hard by the lava walls of Table Mountain, the anvil-shaped butte circumscribed by the Chain Lakes Loop. Elevation gain here is minimal and because the trail is mostly above tree line, Mount Baker views are large and unobstructed.

At **2.0** miles, at the signed intersection with the Ptarmigan Ridge Trail, go right, following the sign for Chain Lakes. Drop about 500 feet over the next mile into a heathered valley of wildflowers, hemlocks, and lakes—first Mazama at **2.75** miles, then Iceberg at **3.0** miles, then Hayes at **3.25** miles; Arbuthnet is behind Hayes, not reached by trail—these are the Chain Lakes. Grab a handful of the tasty mountain blueberries that are everywhere, dip your tootsies in the water, and bask in the mountain magic.

Once you've had enough—and it's very possible you won't reach that point—get back on the trail and climb steadily for about a mile to Herman Saddle at about **4.2** miles. Straight ahead (to the east) you're treated to jagged Mount Shuksan, whose image adorns countless calendars, postcards, and coffee-table books, with good reason. Below are the Bagley Lakes, fed by the permanent snowfield at the foot of Table Mountain.

Descend 1.5 miles—much of it slippery talus—into the basin. At about **5.7** miles cross a stone bridge. The visitors center, about 200 feet above you, is about 0.3 mile ahead.

Going Farther

The Bagley Lakes and Lower Wild Goose Trails (Hike 54) and Fire and Ice Trail can also be accessed from the Heather Meadows Visitors Center. Down the road a way is the Picture Lake loop (Hike 53); a short way up the road is the Lake Ann trailhead (Hike 56); and at road's end is the trailhead for Table Mountain (Hike 58), Ptarmigan Ridge (Hike 59), and Artist Ridge Trail (Hike 57). ■

56. Lake Ann Trail

RATING	DISTANCE	HIKING TIME
★★★★★	8.4 miles round-trip	6 hours

ELEVATION GAIN	HIGH POINT	DIFFICULTY
1,800 feet	4,900 feet to 3,900 feet	◆ ◆ ◆ ◆ ◆

BEST SEASON
Jan Feb Mar Apr May Jun Jul **Aug Sep Oct** Nov Dec

The Hike

Although Mount Baker has a number of day hikes that offer up-close access, Mount Shuksan doesn't. Which is why the Lake Ann Trail rules. No other trail gives you front-row Shuksan seats like this one. Sound effects too—tumbling snowslides on the Curtis Glaciers provide plenty of rumbles.

Getting There

Head east on Highway 542 (Mount Baker Highway) for about 56 miles, about 23 miles east of the Glacier Public Service Center, and 1.5 miles past the Mount Baker Ski Area's upper lodge to the Lake Ann trailhead on the left side of the road. Elevation: 4,700 feet.

The Trail

In a reverse of most trails, start by switchbacking down through forest, dropping about 600 feet over the first mile into the Swift Creek

---

PERMITS/CONTACT
Northwest Forest Pass required/Mount Baker–Snoqualmie National Forest, Glacier Public Service Center, (360) 599-2714

MAPS
USGS Shuksan Arm; Green Trails Mount Shuksan 14

TRAIL NOTES
Leashed dogs okay; kid-friendly; great views

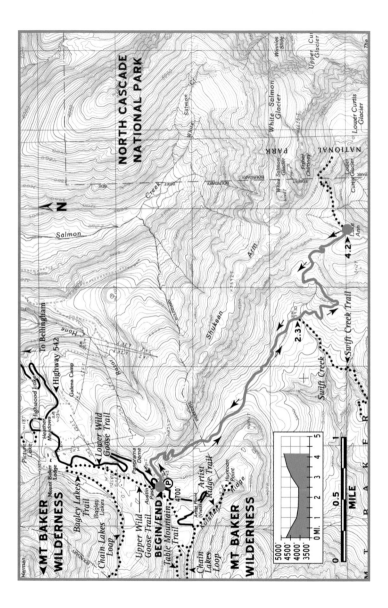

drainage. Tiptoe east through this lush, mostly level, open valley, marveling at waterfalls, creeklets, Shuksan Arm's towering rock wall, and, at the head of this hanging valley, the wonderous ice- and snow-clad Mount Shuksan. When necessary, rock-hop across streams—some of which flow in opposite direction from one another—and at **1.4** miles, reenter forest.

In a little less than a mile, you'll reach Swift Creek, the trail's low point, elevation-wise, at about 3,900 feet. The Swift Creek Trail to the left heads south from here, near the privy sign. Stay straight on the Lake Ann Trail and—once you are across the creek, trekking poles border on must-have status here—begin the 1,000-foot climb immediately, ascending first through forest, then through a mix of rock gardens and open meadows. Views improve with practically every step as Mount Baker, Table Mountain, and that end of the world to the west beg for eyeball-time.

At about **4.0** miles, reach the saddle above Lake Ann at about 4,900 feet. Head down a couple hundred feet in 0.2 mile to explore this deep blue—and likely snow- and/or ice-wrapped—wonder, stunning against its Mount Shuksan backdrop. Lots of great campsites here and, most likely, lots of folks desiring those campsites. Many are climbers heading for the top of Mount Shuksan via the Fisher Chimney route.

Listen as Shuksan's Upper and Lower Curtis Glaciers crack, groan, and moan for attention, often with thunderlike rumbles. Return as you came.

Going Farther

From the lake, a somewhat primitive climbers trail climbs about 400 feet and takes you about 0.75 mile closer to the headwall. Proceed only if it's snow free. The Swift Creek Trail at about 2.3 miles is obscure and unmaintained.

Down the road a way is the trailhead for Bagley Lakes and Lower Wild Goose Trails (Hike 54) and Chain Lakes Loop (Hike 55); down the road farther is the Picture Lake loop (Hike 53); and at road's end is the trailhead for Table Mountain (Hike 58), Ptarmigan Ridge (Hike 59), and Artist Ridge Trail (Hike 57). ■

57. Artist Ridge Trail

RATING	DISTANCE	HIKING TIME
★★★★☆	1-mile lollipop loop	45 minutes

ELEVATION GAIN	HIGH POINT	DIFFICULTY
170 feet	5,250 feet	◆◇◇◇◇

BEST SEASON											
Jan	Feb	Mar	Apr	May	Jun	**Jul**	**Aug**	**Sep**	**Oct**	Nov	Dec

The Hike

Artist Ridge boasts the highest quotient of awesome-views-for-least-effort of any trail in this book. Both Mounts Baker and Shuksan are larger than large, and interpretive signage along this partially paved trail tells the story of what you're looking at—alpine magic of the highest order.

Getting There

Head east on Highway 542 (Mount Baker Highway) for about 58 miles to the road-end parking lot at Artist Point, about 25 miles east of the Glacier Public Service Center. Elevation: 5,100 feet.

The Trail

Find the paved trailhead and map kiosk at the southeast corner of the Artist Point parking lot. The first 50 yards of the trail are paved and lead to a scenic viewpoint. Check out your surroundings with

---

PERMITS/CONTACT
Northwest Forest Pass required/Mount Baker–Snoqualmie National Forest, Glacier Public Service Center, (360) 599-2714

MAPS
USGS Shuksan Arm; Green Trails Mount Shuksan 14

TRAIL NOTES
Leashed dogs okay; kid-friendly; great views

View of Shuksan Arm from Huntoon Point

your personal IMAX vision and scope out the Nooksack Ridge, Mount Shuksan, Mount Baker, Table Mountain, Mount Herman, and all the nooks and crannies that are the North Cascades.

To continue, follow the gravel trail to the left as it rides along the Kulshan Ridge for about 0.5 mile. Mount Shuksan, big, bold, and beautiful, is straight ahead at all times. Minor ups and downs, ins and outs amid boulders offer some variety. As do patches of snow, or downright snowdrifts, which seem to linger here forever some years.

Shuksan Arm is the nearby ridge across the basin to the east. Follow its spine with your eyes as it climbs, then glaciates, then turns to rock, then becomes the summit pyramid of the North Cascades'

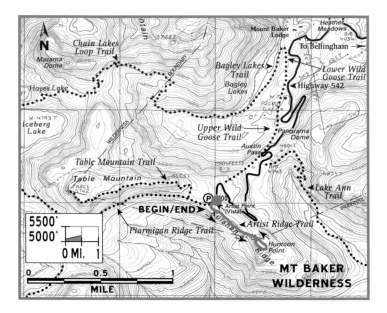

most popular pin-up. Below to the right, follow the thread of the Lake Ann Trail (Hike 56).

The Artist Ridge Trail meanders through a small talus slope, finally ending with a small loop at Huntoon Point that offers a number of big boulders on which to lunch, snooze, or just count the peaks. On the way back, Mount Baker and Table Mount dominate the sky.

Going Farther

The trailheads for Table Mountain (Hike 58) and Ptarmigan Ridge (Hike 59) are at the southwest corner of the Artist Point parking lot. Down the road 2 miles is the Lake Ann trailhead (Hike 56); down the road 3 miles is the trailhead for Bagley Lakes and Lower Wild Goose Trails (Hike 54) and Chain Lakes Loop (Hike 55); and down the road 4 miles is the Picture Lake loop (Hike 53). ■

58. Table Mountain

RATING	DISTANCE	HIKING TIME
★★★★☆	3 miles round-trip	1 hour

ELEVATION GAIN	HIGH POINT	DIFFICULTY
600 feet	5,700 feet	♦♦♦♦♦

BEST SEASON
Jan Feb Mar Apr May Jun **Jul Aug Sep Oct** Nov Dec

The Hike

Talk about a trail being short and sweet—no trail in this book gives you as much mountain-vista bang for your hiking buck. Stunning 360-degree North Cascades views are yours without nary breaking a sweat. One caution: The narrow trail up feels a bit exposed, so don't be shy; hug the rock wall if you feel the need.

Getting There

Head east on Highway 542 (Mount Baker Highway) for about 58 miles to the road-end Artist Point parking lot, about 25 miles east of the Glacier Public Service Center. Elevation: 5,100 feet.

The Trail

From the southwest end of the Artist Point parking lot (the side nearest Mount Baker), find the map kiosk detailing the area's trails. Because snow almost always lingers here throughout the summer,

PERMITS/CONTACT
Northwest Forest Pass required/Mount Baker–Snoqualmie National Forest, Glacier Public Service Center, (360) 599-2714

MAPS
USGS Shuksan Arm; Green Trails Mount Shuksan 14

TRAIL NOTES
No dogs; great views

Snowfield atop Table Mountain

chances are that signs will be posted pointing the way to the Table Mountain and Chain Lakes Trails. Follow the sign for Table Mountain, crossing a short stretch of snow (likely), rock, and meadow.

Then start a short but steep climb, some of it in the form of rock steps. Careful not to kick rocks down on folks below you. And there will be folks below you, especially on weekends—this is a very popular trail. If you bring small children, hold their hands and don't let go. At **0.4** mile reach Table Mountain's flat top and spin around, letting your personal IMAX vision take in countless peaks, glaciers, valleys, and meadows. Mounts Baker and Shuksan look close enough to touch and the Nooksack Ridge, Baker Lake, the Pickets, and a bunch of other North Cascades all-stars are not much farther away. Down below, check out the Bagley Lakes and the maze of trails snaking throughout the whole Heather Meadows area.

From here, wander west following trail when the snow level allows, cairns and boot track otherwise. Because there are permanent snowfields on Table's plateau top, it's never completely free of snow. Pick a rock, break out the picnic basket, and enjoy the stunning views. Careful not to wander too close to the edge, for there are dangerous

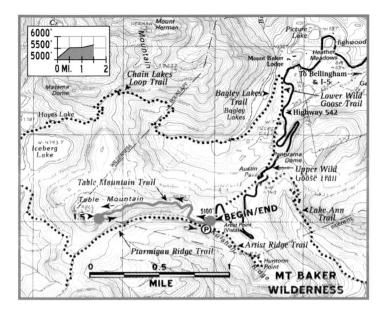

drops on all sides. At about **1.5** miles, the trail/route peters out at the west end of Table Mountain. Return the same way.

Going Farther

The Artist Ridge Trail (Hike 57), also accessed from the Artist Point parking area, is a nice companion trail to Table Mountain. The Chain Lakes Loop (Hike 55) and Ptarmigan Ridge Trails (Hike 59) are also accessed from the same trailhead as Table Mountain.

Down the road 2 miles is the Lake Ann trailhead (Hike 56); down the road 3 miles is the trailhead for Bagley Lakes and Lower Wild Goose Trails (Hike 54); and down the road 4 miles is the Picture Lake loop (Hike 53). ∎

59. Ptarmigan Ridge Trail

RATING	DISTANCE	HIKING TIME
★ ★ ★ ★ ★	12 miles round-trip	8 hours
ELEVATION GAIN	**HIGH POINT**	**DIFFICULTY**
2,250 feet	6,450 feet	◆ ◆ ◆ ◆ ◇

BEST SEASON
Jan Feb Mar Apr May Jun Jul **Aug Sep Oct** Nov Dec

The Trail

Pure, unadulterated mountain magic—that's Ptarmigan Ridge. Throughout, Mounts Baker and Shuksan—Mother Nature's master-pieces in the rock, ice, and snow mediums—lure you along the ridge or are at your shoulder whispering sweet nothings. Ptarmigan Ridge just might be my favorite, especially in late summer when enough snow has melted that you can hike almost to the Portals.

Note: This trail is in the high country and is one of the last to be free of snow. Thus, although the views are picture-postcard perfect, the Ptarmigan Ridge Trail is rugged in parts and always requires some stretches of snow travel.

Getting There

Head east on Highway 542 (Mount Baker Highway) for about 58 miles to the road-end parking lot at Artist Point, about 25 miles east of the Glacier Public Service Center. Elevation: 5,100 feet.

PERMITS/CONTACT
Northwest Forest Pass required/Mount Baker–Snoqualmie National Forest, Glacier Public Service Center, (360) 599-2714

MAPS
USGS Mount Baker, Shuksan Arm; Green Trails Mount Shuksan 14

TRAIL NOTES
Leashed dogs okay; great views

A ridge with a view

The Trail

At the parking area, head toward the southeast corner (Mount Baker side) and the map kiosk. Follow the sign for Chain Lakes/ Ptarmigan Ridge Trails—not Table Mountain—and begin a mostly level traverse hard by Table Mountain's southern walls. Most likely, your jaw will involuntarily drop at the unobstructed Mount Baker views before you, but trust me: they keep getting better and better. Check out that tilted, spikelike spire protruding from the ridge to the left. That's Coleman Pinnacle, and you'll be passing just below that in a few hours.

At **1.2** miles, reach a signed intersection with the Ptarmigan Ridge Trail. Go left here and head directly for Mount Baker. Almost instantly the trail becomes more rugged, drops down for a bit, then spreads out far ahead of you, drenched as it is by the permanent snowfields near the top of the ridge to your left. Speaking of snowfields, at about **2.1** miles, climb a short, steep, snowy stretch that puts you

Crevasses on Mount Baker's north side

right on the ridge. If you're not comfortable, don't proceed. Carrying an ice ax or trekking poles is advised.

Follow the ridge trail—your personal mountain-magic carpet ride—for as far as the snow level allows. Mount Shuksan, flanked by the Nooksack Ridge to the left and the Pickets to the right, demands shout-outs. Ahead, Mount Baker appears to rise larger and larger, as if it's being inflated by a massive bicycle pump, its

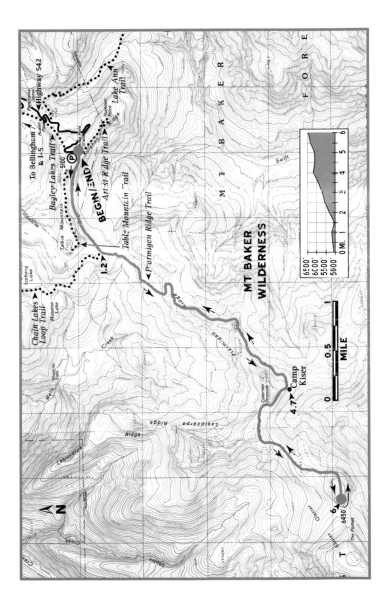

individual glaciers defined and distinct. Rainbow and Park Glaciers dominate, and, depending how far the snow level allows, you'll pass just above the Sholes Glacier. The trail, which crosses snowfields, talus slopes, as well as wildflower-raging meadows, gains elevation but for the most part, does so gradually.

At about **4.7** miles, reach the Camp Kiser area, a mostly level and popular camping area below Coleman Pinnacle. In a valley to the south, look for an unnamed icy lake of otherworldly blue. Look for mountain goats too. From here, continue on as far as the snow and your comfort levels allow.

The trail soon enters a rocky moonscape and is hard to follow. Scramble up a rocky hump that butts up against the Sholes Glacier (close enough to touch) and continue following cairns or boot track another mile or so to the top of a rocky outcropping, where you can go no farther. How do you know you can go no farther? Because to take another step would result in a several-hundred-foot fall. You've reached the Portals. Return the way you came.

Going Farther

The Artist Point parking lot is also the trailhead for the Chain Lakes Loop (Hike 55), Table Mountain (Hike 58), and Artist Ridge Trail (Hike 57).

Down the road 2 miles is the Lake Ann trailhead (Hike 56); down the road 3 miles is the trailhead for Bagley Lakes and Lower Wild Goose Trails (Hike 54); and down the road 4 miles is the Picture Lake loop (Hike 53). ■

INDEX

ABOUT THE AUTHOR

MIKE MCQUAIDE has written outdoor, travel, and lifestyle stories for everyone from *Outside* and *Sunset* to *Runner's World*, *Adventure Cyclist*, and more. A former outdoors writer for the *Seattle Times*, Mike has written six books on outdoor recreation and travel including *Day Hike! Central Cascades* and *75 Classic Rides: Washington*. He is also an avid cyclist—both road and mountain bike—as well as a trail runner, mountaineer, and snowboarder. He's been hiking and running Pacific Northwest trails for more than twenty-five years. Mike currently lives in Luxembourg with his wife, Jennifer, and son, Baker, named for the mountain. Follow his adventures at www.facebook.com/anamericaninluxembourg.